Titles in the **Discovering Civil War America** series:

The Battle Between the Farm Lanes:

Hancock Saves the Union Center, Gettysburg, July 2, 1863

A HISTORY AND TOUR GUIDE

by
David Shultz and David Wieck

Volume 4 in The Discovering Civil War America Series

David Shultz and David Wieck
The Battle Between the Farm Lanes
Hancock Saves the Union Center
Gettysburg, July 2, 1863

Library of Congress Cataloging-in-Publication Data

Shultz, Dave.
  The battle between the farm lanes : Hancock saves the
Union center, July second, 1863 : a history and tour guide /
by David Shultz and David Wieck.
      p. cm. -- (Discovering Civil War America series ; v. 4)
  Includes bibliographical references and index.
  ISBN 0-9673770-7-2
1. Gettysburg, Battle of, Gettysburg, Pa., 1863. 2. Hancock,
Winfield Scott, 1824-1886--Military leadership. 3. Com-
mand of troops--Case studies. 4. United States. Army--
History--Civil War, 1861-1865. 5. Gettysburg National
Military Park (Pa.)--Tours. I. Wieck, David, 1947- II. Title.
  E475.53.S554 2006
  973.7'349--dc22
  2006021602

Printed in the United States 0f America

Ironclad Publishing, Inc.
6956 East Broad Street, #224
Columbus, OH 43213

Table of Contents

Acknowledgments

We would like to thank many individuals and institutions for their generous assistance received while preparing this study. Unfortunately our memories are such that we are unable to recollect everyone whose commitment made our work so much easier. To those we overlook, our sincere apologies.

Foremost, we would like to thank the staffs of the National Archives & Records Administration, Washington, D.C., the Readers Services Department, Huntington Library, San Marino, California, the Special Collections Library, United States Military Academy, West Point New York, and the United States Geological Survey, Denver, Colorado. Without their professional assistance this study could not have been undertaken. We are thankful to all the repositories and libraries whose opened doors made the work so much easier.

Our thanks for his gracious assistance to the late Jacob Sheads who, in 1963, while conducting a private tour, assured President John F. Kennedy that the First Minnesota did not stop Wilcox's brigade alone and unsupported. The good colonel told that tale a hundred times, which planted the seed 40-odd years ago. A personal thank you to Anna Howeland and Carl Clink of the Civil War Round Table of Orange County, California and to Don Ernsberger, whose knowledge of Hancock is unsurpassed. To our families and friends whose support helped us during lengthy study.

Our thanks, too, to all those historians, amateur and professional, who tramp the battlefields. We firmly believe that the ground, closely observed, can tell us stories. The father of one such person described this activity, with a sniff, as "looking at dirt." Well, that may be. Here's to all of you, like us, who look at dirt and hear its stories.

Lastly, this work could not have been presented without help from the late Richard Rollins. It was from his vertical files that most of the documentation came. It was he who suggested we work this project, knowing that what we had would add clarity to the bigger picture.

Illustrations

List of Maps

NOTES:
Hancock's Ride is overlaid on a 1939 United States
Geological Survey aerial photograph.

The Maps for the Driving and Walking Tour are overlaid on
USGS topographical survey maps.

Driving & Walking Tour Photos

Foreword

The Second Corps of the Army of the Potomac arrived on the Gettysburg battlefield during the morning of July 2, 1863. As the hours passed these Union veterans filed into position on Cemetery Ridge from Ziegler's Grove south toward Little Round Top. About 2:00 P.M., the officers and men watched as their comrades in Major General Daniel E. Sickles's Third Corps marched west, uncovering the left flank of the Second Corps on Cemetery Ridge. Sickles's unauthorized movement heralded a terrible reckoning.

The whirlwind struck at four o'clock when two infantry divisions of Lieutenant General James Longstreet's Confederate First Corps of the Army of Northern Virginia attacked. For the next three hours the fighting engulfed the southern end of the battlefield from Little Round Top, into Devil's Den, across Houck's Ridge and the Wheatfield, to the Peach Orchard, and then north into the fields adjoining Emmitsburg Road. The Confederate assault crushed the Union salient at the Peach Orchard, seized control of Devil's Den, lapped up the slopes of Little Round Top, and wrenched a section of Emmitsburg Road from Sickles's troops.

From Cemetery Ridge, Major General Winfield Scott Hancock, commander of the Second Corps, looked on as the shattered ranks of the Third Corps flowed rearward across the fields. The army's finest corps commander, who always seemed to be dressed for an officer's ball, Hancock began shifting units toward the oncoming enemy lines. One division hurried south and into the Wheatfield maelstrom. Along Emmitsburg Road additional brigades from the Confederate Third Corps moved to the attack. If the center of the Union army's line was to be held, it would rest primarily with Hancock's veterans in infantry regiments and artillery batteries.

The members of the Second Corps were among the finest, if not the best, combat troops in the Union army. A few of the regiments had fought at First Bull Run, others had participated in the debacle at Ball's Bluff, more had held firm in the retreat across the Peninsula during the Seven Days' Campaign, and many had bled and died in West Woods and along Bloody Lane at Antietam and had been slaughtered before the stone wall at Fredericksburg. The corps had been spared from the worst of the fighting at Chancellorsville. It had been months, then, since the December 1862 day at Fredericksburg, a time of waiting for these survivors to exact an accounting from their foes. It would come on the afternoon of this hot July day.

Some of the fiercest and most critical fighting occurred in a sector of the battlefield framed by the farm lanes of Abraham Trostle and Jacob Hummelbaugh homesteads. In this area a dozen Second Corps regiments—units from Massachusetts, Minnesota, New York, Pennsylvania, and Vermont—and thirty-seven gun crews from seven batteries opposed the Southerners in a series of attacks and counterattacks. Hancock and his subordinates ordered these regiments into the cauldron, plugging gaps in the line and buying time until more Federals arrived to secure the beleaguered Union position.

It is this fury between the Trostle and Hummelbaugh

farms that David Shultz and David Wieck chronicle in this
book. Their detailed account of the action and the accompanying driving and walking tour of the ground are a worthy
addition to the vast body of work on the July 1863 battle. Gettysburg brought redemption for the Army of the Potomac.
Hancock and the Second Corps shouldered a crucial role in
the engagement's outcome.

                                        Jeffry D. Wert

Major General Winfield S. Hancock
National Archives, Washington D.C.

Prologue | Philadelphia, Pa. July 7, 1863

Major General Hancock desires to know the designation of a certain regiment, and the name of its commander, belonging to the First, Second, or Twelfth Corps, which, at the insistence of General Hancock, charged a rebel regiment which had passed through our lines on Thursday evening, 2nd Instant. The conduct of this regiment and its commander were so marked in this as in the subsequent advance in line of battle, that General Hancock desires properly to notice the subject.

> W. G. Mitchell.
> Aide-de-Camp, and
> Assistant Adjutant General.[1]

The above circular was issued to the Army of the Potomac at the order of Maj. Gen. Winfield Scott Hancock four days after the battle of Gettysburg. Recuperating from a terrible wound in his lower abdomen that he had received on July Third, Hancock lay in his Philadelphia hospital bed thinking, not of July Third and Pickett's Charge, but of July Second and the extraordinary performance of a regiment whose identity he still did not know. What regiment was this? Who was its commander? As we can see from the circular, he did not even know the brigade, division, or corps the regiment belonged to.

Legend has it that this regiment was Col. William Colvill, Jr.'s 1st Minnesota Volunteer Regiment, First Brigade, Second Division, Second Corps. According to the legend, the 262 officers and men of the 1st Minnesota charged and stopped an entire brigade, numbering 1700 men, under the command of Brig. Gen. Cadmus M. Wilcox.

On the afternoon of July Second, Lt. Gen. James Longstreet's massive assault struck the Union left, crushed the advanced position of Maj. Gen. Daniel E. Sickles's Third Corps, and rolled northward up the Federal line. On Longstreet's left, Wilcox's men joined in the assault. As the Union line crumbled, a huge gap opened in the center. Wilcox's men forcibly crossed over the Emmitsburg Road heading toward that gaping hole, pressing all those before them. The Taneytown Road, an important supply line for the Army of the Potomac, lay just beyond the low ridge to Wilcox's front, with no apparent defender between his line and its crest.

"Hancock rode up and, reining his horse to a sudden stop, looked about for infantry to throw into the breach. 'My God,' he allegedly exclaimed, pointing to the 1st Minnesota, 'Are these all the men we have here?'"[2] According to Lt. William Lochren of the 1st Minnesota, "Hancock spurred to where we stood, calling out as he reached us, 'What regiment is this?' 'First Minnesota,' replied Colvill. 'Charge those lines!' commanded Hancock."[3] "Advance, Colonel, and take those colors," is how Colvill remembered the order.

Was it the 1st Minnesota who alone checked and stopped the Confederate tide until Union reinforcements arrived? Was this the regiment Hancock referred to in his circular? For the answers to these questions, we must look beyond Colvill and Lieutenant Lochren to the surrounding events of July 2.

Chapter 1 | July Second: Hancock's Second Corps Arrives

Peering from beneath the twisted bill of his worn kepi, Capt. Dunbar R. Ransom, commander of the First Regular Brigade of Reserve Artillery, raised his field glasses to his eyes. From his vantage point just east of the crest of a long, low ridge, he scanned the surrounding area. He stood in the midst of good Pennsylvania farmland, black earth, with fields of wheat and corn, and orchards brimming with apples, peaches, and cherries. Stands of woods, alternating with pastures and grazing meadows, were also dotted with stone and clapboard farmhouses and large ornate barns. Ransom stood on a ridge that rose gently, ending in a hill to the north, and on that hill were thousands of Union troops, members of the First and Eleventh Corps of the Army of the Potomac, who had retreated to the high ground late on the afternoon of July First. In the cemetery on that hill, gun limbers, carriages, and caissons, were in battery and parked amongst the tombstones and family plots. A coppice of trees was visible on the heights and north of that coppice, not a half-mile distant, lay the town of Gettysburg, occupied by Gen. Robert E. Lee's Army of Northern Virginia.

To the west was another ridge, reaching away to the south,

topped by a Lutheran seminary nestled in a grove of trees at its northern end. It was a ridge like countless others in this part of the state, no different from them until yesterday, when men in blue and gray had swarmed over it, and died by the thousands. A shallow valley ran between the two ridges, and through it the road connecting the town of Emmitsburg, Maryland, approximately 10 miles distant, with the Adams County seat of Gettysburg. Three avenues converged on Gettysburg from the south, the Emmitsburg Road to the west of Cemetery Ridge, the winding Taneytown Road to the east, and, further east still, a broad turnpike that led south-southeast to Baltimore.

Shifting his gaze, Ransom scanned the valley to the east of Cemetery Ridge. The red morning sun had not yet cleared the next ridge to the east, leaving the valley's floor partially concealed in shadow. A blanket of mist and lingering camp-fire smoke drifted through hollows, wood lots, and orchards. The distinctive smells of battle and of an army in camp permeated the sultry morning air.

Ransom focused on the darkened silhouette of a small tract of woods just beyond a hill a quarter mile south and east of his position.[1] A wooded knoll west of Taneytown Road blocked much of his view but, just beyond an intersection with a lane leading west past a granite schoolhouse, a cloud of dust billowed in the pre-dawn light.

Moments earlier, several companies of pioneers belonging to Maj. Gen. Winfield Scott Hancock's Second Corps had double-timed past, angling northwest up the gentle eastern slope of Cemetery Ridge. Looking over his shoulder,

Ransom could see these men, detached from the 14th Indiana Infantry and commanded by Capt. Nathan Willard, already dismantling the rail and snake fences belonging to local farmers Jacob Hummelbaugh and tenant Peter Frey.[2] Clearing the fences would allow following troops to move easily and quickly once they left the road.

The dust cloud noted by Ransom was being kicked up by the feet of Union soldiers moving back onto the Taneytown Road just south of its intersection with the Granite Schoolhouse Road. Hancock's Second Corps was on the move. These men had bivouacked beyond the southern end of Cemetery Ridge, southeast of a rocky round-topped hill referred to then as Sugar Loaf Mountain, and later as Little Round Top. Rousted from sleep between 2:30 and 3:00 A.M. to a breakfast of coffee and hardtack, they hit the road about 4:15 A.M.—before first light. Their march toward Gettysburg along the narrow fence-lined Taneytown Road was tortuous as they almost immediately became entangled in debris from Maj. Gen. Oliver O. Howard's Eleventh Corps, which had passed through the day before. The road was hemmed in by fenced lots, small woods, and the ever-present stone walls. Numerous fenced and walled intersecting rural lanes, running perpendicular to the road, made cross-country marching almost impossible, and a huge traffic jam ensued within moments of the Second Corps' falling-in.[3]

Hancock's column struggled up the road for over an hour, until about 5:30 A.M., when the leading elements, belonging to Brig. Gen. Alexander Hays's Third Division, were ordered off the road to the right, after managing only about a mile and a half of difficult marching.[4] Filing into the wood lots and open fields belonging to local farmers Michael Schriber and William Patterson, Hays's men were held in readiness immediately south of the Granite Schoolhouse Road, while Brig. Gen. John Gibbon's Second Division, and Brig. Gen. John Caldwell's First Division, closed up.

The Taneytown Road was alive with everything imaginable known to battle. Besides the few citizens scurrying south, the narrow lane was crawling with couriers, orderlies and adjutants. Detachments and cavalry squadrons dashed about, and, as with armies everywhere, soldiers either moved in a great hurry or not at all. Many men who had become separated from their units huddled in small groups. Having fallen out during the march, too hot or tired or sick or footsore to keep up, they were now trying to search out and reunite with their comrades. Hancock had held his Second Corps at Uniontown, Maryland, for a few extra hours on June 29th to let his men close up—more than three-quarters of them had fallen out during the exhausting march. They had slogged through rain and heat and mud and dust for the better part of five days, rarely resting for more than a few hours at a time. The ever-present fugitives skulked about as well, trying to look as if they belonged to one unit or another. The Provost Marshal's guard, the police of the Army of the Potomac, moved among them, trying to sort out the skulkers from the stragglers.[5]

Conspicuous by its absence, and noted by Captain Ransom, was wagon traffic. It was evident that everything with wheels, save artillery carriages and caissons, had been ordered off the road. Artillery baggage wagons and ambulances were no exception. As of 4:30 A.M., the Taneytown Road had been declared off limits to most wheeled traffic. Even the much-needed ammunition train that accompanied Captain Ransom's Regular Artillery Brigade and which had been promised to Howard's Eleventh Corps would sit for four hours in its park south of Little Round Top. Maj. Gen. George G. Meade, the commander of the Army of the Potomac, had directed the expediting of this small ammunition train. Without clearing it with Meade, Hancock dispatched a verbal communiqué from his headquarters below Little Round Top to clear the road of all wagon traffic, no exceptions. No one dared challenge Hancock's order, however informal, least of all Captain Ransom, who had ridden ahead of his column to await the ammunition train. Like others, he had no choice but to wait. Captain Ransom lowered his glasses and reached for his timepiece; it was nearly 6:00 A.M.

Maintaining control of the Taneytown Road was imperative to the Army of the Potomac. By 6:00 A.M. all other corps then converging on Gettysburg had been directed to the Baltimore Pike, a much better and broader avenue, leaving the ammunition and supply trains free use of the Taneytown Road. If the army was to hold the positions laid out by Meade that morning, the Taneytown Road and Cemetery Ridge to its west had to be held at all costs. The ridge was key to Meade's planned deployment in that it screened his troops, their reinforcements, supplies, numbers, and movements. It also screened his direct link to Frederick City, Westminster, and Baltimore beyond, and was critical to his ability to move troops, materièl, and supplies. Holding the small round-topped mountain that anchored the left, or southern end, of the line was as important as holding Cemetery Ridge. If any of these critical heights were lost, even for a brief period of time, the crowded Taneytown Road would be in jeopardy. This in turn would place too much pressure on the already overcrowded Baltimore Pike, Meade's foremost concern.[6]

While Nathan Willard's pioneers pulled down fences on the ridge north of Ransom, Hays's division reentered the Taneytown Road from its temporary haven south of the Granite Schoolhouse Road. The captain watched Hays's column approach from a point near the intersection of Jacob Hummelbaugh's farm lane and the Taneytown Road. Peter Frey's large stone home stood a quarter-mile north of the intersection, and Meade's army headquarters were 500 yards beyond that.[7]

Brig. Gen. Alexander Hays
National Archives

Hays's column of foot-sore men, their blouses, kepis, and hats coated with fine Pennsylvania dust, closed on Hummelbaugh's farm lane shortly after sunrise. Although it had been light for nearly an hour, the sun had yet to crest the ridge east of Taneytown Road.[8] The column was unusually quiet this morning. Aside from the occasional barking of an officer, all that could be heard were the tramping of feet, the rattling of accouterments, the jingling and clanking of equipment, a cough or faint remark here and there. These were the familiar sounds of veterans moving to battle, who knew what to expect and did not need officers to remind them what to do. Morale was high in Hays's Third Brigade, in fact throughout the Second Corps. They had confidence in Hancock. They knew him to be tough and smart and competent under pressure. While there was something careerist about Hancock, his men trusted him, even loved him in their soldiers' way. They would follow him to hell if asked, and he would gladly lead them.[9]

At that moment, Hancock was in conversation at army headquarters. He had ridden ahead and was handed a map indicating where each corps was to be positioned upon its arrival. This map laid out the commanding general's exact plan of how he expected to hold the Taneytown Road and, even more importantly, the Baltimore Pike. The former avenue would be secured by fortifying Cemetery Ridge beginning below West Cemetery Hill and running south two miles toward Little Round Top. The position began with portions of the First and Eleventh Corps on Cemetery Hill; Hancock's Second Corps would be next in line, followed by Maj. Gen. Daniel Sickles's Third Corps. Sickles was to anchor his right flank near the Hummelbaugh farm lane, connecting with Hancock's left. Sickles's left would in turn be anchored about three-quarters of a mile south, near the Trostle farm lane, connecting with the right of the Fifth Corps under Maj. Gen. George Sykes.[10] The Fifth Corps was to anchor the left wing of the Army, with its own left secured at Little Round Top.

Meanwhile, Sickles was holding his own staff meeting. He had two problems. With two brigades from his First Division, commanded by Maj. Gen. David Birney, dispatched to cover the far left until Sykes came up, Sickles's Second Division, commanded by Brig. Gen. Andrew A. Humphreys, was too small to cover the position assigned him on Meade's map, which stretched along Cemetery Ridge from Hummelbaugh's farm lane south to the Fairfield Cross Road below Little Round Top. He also didn't like the look of the high ground—the Emmitsburg Road Rise—to his front. For reasons never clearly explained, Sickles had already decided not to occupy the position on the ridge that Hancock and Meade thought he would and was advancing his troops to the high ground to his front.

If Hancock knew Sickles's people were not yet in the position on the ridge indicated on Meade's map, he did not mention it at the time. Hancock's assigned position began at the Hummelbaugh farm lane and, without Humphreys's men on his left, his flank was "in the air," open and unsupported. With Sickles's Corps advanced, Hancock's line would be exposed to potential flanking and envelopment, and his line could be rolled up. Hancock had been assured, however, that Humphreys's Division would pull back from the low ground along Plum Run and connect with his left. It appears he gave little further thought to Cemetery Ridge south of the Hummelbaugh farm, focusing instead on what was to his front.[11]

Chapter 2 | Hancock Secures Cemetery Ridge

The footsore men of Hancock's Second Corps paid little attention to the large gathering of officers near the Hummelbaugh intersection as they passed through it, with Hays's division leading the way. They continued north on Taneytown Road, moving toward the huge gaps in the rail and stone fences made by Willard's pioneers.[1]

Brigadier Generals Henry J. Hunt, Chief of Artillery, Army of the Potomac, and Robert O. Tyler, commander of the Artillery Reserve, watched with Captain Ransom as Hays's column passed through the intersection. Capt. John G. Hazard, commanding the Second Corps Artillery Brigade, joined them with several of his staff. Hunt and Hazard were talking when Hays's lead unit, Col. Samuel S. Carroll's First Brigade, angled into the fields west of Taneytown Road. Carroll in turn was followed by Col. Thomas Smyth's Second Brigade, which also entered Hummelbaugh's meadow, crossing over the crumbling stone wall north of the intersection and ascending the gentle slope of the ridge, angling toward a small copse of trees in the distance.[2] Hunt asked Ransom for the time. It was about 6:30.[3]

Col. George L. Willard's Third Brigade waited in the road for the rear of Smyth's column to clear the intersection. The

Colonel George L. Willard
National Archives

boredom and fatigue of the long march fell away as shells began passing and exploding overhead. Two of Captain Hazard's batteries pulled out of line behind Willard's column and with cannoneers running, came hustling past the brigade. They were 1st Lt. George A. Woodruff's Battery I, 1st United States Light Artillery, and Capt. William A. Arnold's Battery A, 1st Rhode Island Light Artillery. They followed Col. Edward Warner, Inspector General of the Army of the Potomac and Hunt's chief of staff, to a farm lane north of the opening in the fence, then turned west along the narrow lane, past the Peter Frey farmhouse, and up toward the crest of the ridge. Just south of the copse of trees on the western crest of the ridge, Warner reported to General Hays, who took possession of the guns.[4] With the sun behind them, they were clearly visible to the gray–clad gunners on Seminary Ridge, who promptly opened on them. Smyth's column was moving past the trees at this moment, and both his brigade and Warner's two batteries came under fire.

By now Hazard had finished his discussion with Hunt and had arrived on the scene. He placed his two batteries in the positions indicated to him by Hays, west of and below the crest of the low ridge, so as not to expose the infantry east of them to counter-battery fire. Placing batteries in front of one's infantry in the face of the enemy on an open crest would almost always invite a concentrated counter-battery fire that frequently passed through or over the intended target, striking troops to the rear. Counter-battery fire against these two batteries never amounted to much, however, and Hays's first two brigades took their positions without further incident.

The six Napoleons of Lieutenant Woodruff's 1st U.S. Light swung about in "Reverse Trot," his six smoothbores forming "Action Front" 100 yards north of a small whitewashed clapboard barn. Placed in the open below the western edge of Ziegler's Grove, they drew the immediate attention of Confederate artillery near the McMillan farm as well as small arms fire from skirmishers and sharpshooters near Long Lane.[5] Despite this, Woodruff's position was well chosen. Dwellings of another farm belonging to Emanuel Trostle screened his right front from the more numerous enemy batteries nearer the Lutheran Seminary and along the Fairfield Road, allowing Woodruff to concentrate on the Emmitsburg Road to his immediate front and left and not worry about enemy threats to his right.[6]

Captain Arnold's six Three-Inch Ordnance Rifles were placed about 250 yards south of Woodruff to the left of Smyth's brigade. Smyth had moved his men forward to a crumbling stone wall and Battery A's right gun was approximately 100 yards south[7] of farmer Abram Bryan's barn.[8] The rest of his battery stretched southward across the front of Bryan's large orchard toward the copse of trees. The same crumbled stone wall that Smyth's men occupied ran the length of the battery's front, giving Arnold's cannoneers a small but comfortable redoubt.

The regiments of Carroll's First Brigade moved along the crest and took position in woods belonging to a farmer named Ziegler, north of Bryan's small farm, located 320 yards north of the copse of trees.[3] Smyth's brigade was placed south of Carroll in Bryan's peach orchard atop and east of the crest, his skirmishers taking control of a stone wall to Arnold's right that stretched north to Bryan's small clapboard barn.

Chapter 3 | The Harpers Ferry Cowards

Willard's arriving brigade was placed "by battalions en masse" in an open area north of the Bryan peach orchard, his right resting near Smyth's left. First to stack arms east of the crest was the 126th New York, separated from Arnold's parked caissons by a stone wall paralleling the eastern brow of the ridge. The 125th, 111th, and 39th settled in behind them in turn.[1] In all, the four regiments numbered 1,508 officers and men. Since Willard's men were the last to arrive, they were placed in reserve directly behind Arnold's battery—in line to receive the counter-battery fire infantrymen hated so much.[2] The bad luck of the "Harpers Ferry Cowards" still hung over them.[3]

The Army of the Potomac was full of tough units, men who had fought well and bravely but who had not always been well or bravely led. Perhaps more than any units in this army, these four regiments had something to prove, especially the seasoned 39th, also known as the Garibaldi Guards. These veterans had four battles under their belts. The 111th, 125th, and 126th, on the other hand, had only been in uniform for three weeks when they were thrown into battle at Harpers Ferry, beginning September 12, 1862, where these rookies faced none other than Thomas "Stonewall" Jackson and his "Foot Cavalry."

By September 15th, the siege of Harpers Ferry was over. On that dismal day, all four of Willard's New York regiments surrendered their arms and their honor. Nine months later they still bore the stigma of that surrender and the humiliating nickname "Harpers Ferry Cowards." It had been the maiden battle for all but the 39th who, transferred to Harpers Ferry, had arrived on the first day of the fighting. Every man in that regiment felt betrayed by the new recruits. The 39th had fought at First Manassas, Cross Keys, and Middletown—the latter two in the Shenandoah Valley—and had done well. They were a trusted veteran regiment, and their surrender at Harpers Ferry with the 111th, 125th, and 126th was a bitter blow, the sting of which they carried with them to Gettysburg. There was tension in these ranks—the men of the 39th blamed their fellow New Yorkers for their capture.

Although the 111th New York had not been singled out for particular acts of cowardice, it still shared the nickname of "Harpers Ferry Cowards" with the 125th and 126th, guilty by association. Organized as an overflow unit of enlisted men from Cayuga and Wayne Counties, it mustered into service at Albany, New York, August 20, 1862. The 111th New York numbered 22 officers and 368 enlisted men armed with .58 caliber Enfields on the firing line.[4]

Col. Clinton MacDougall had commanded the 111th New York when it surrendered at Harpers Ferry. While he shared in the disgrace of his men, he rejected the idea that he or they were cowards. He knew they were good men. Educated, light-hearted, and forceful, the dashing MacDougall had taken his capture and parole somewhat philosophically. He knew the 111th, 125th, and 126th should not have been in the front lines after negligible training and only three weeks of service. At the same time, he refused to make excuses for the surrender. Like Maj. Hugo Hildebrandt, commander of the 39th, MacDougall was looking for redemption and peace of mind. [5]

Col. Clinton D. MacDougall
National Archives

With the arrival of these regiments, Hancock's right was now secured. Carroll's brigade anchored the right of Hays's division, connecting with the left of Brig. Gen. Henry Baxter's Second Brigade, First Corps, in Zeigler's Woods. Almost immediately, skirmishers from the First and Second Brigades deployed westward, facing the crackle of musketry and rising puffs of smoke that marked encounters with hidden Confederate marksmen scattered in the open areas between the ridges.

Shortly after Carroll and Smyth's skirmishers ventured west, the firing along the Emmitsburg Road escalated into a small but vicious firefight. Within a quarter hour of stacking arms, the entire 39th New York and several companies of the 125th and 126th were reformed and sent forward. Shaking out

into a skirmish line along the Emmitsburg Road, they immediately engaged Confederate riflemen on the William Bliss
property. The rest of Willard's brigade lay down to the rear of
Battery A, exposed to slow but methodical artillery fire from
Seminary Ridge, most of which passed overhead harmlessly.
A few rounds, however, found their mark, exploding above
the brigade on the reverse slope where they lay concealed between the copse of trees and Bryan's farmyard.[6]

MacDougall grew restless while the artillery banged
away and the crackle of musketry grew louder. Accompanied
by his aide, Lt. Col. Isaac Lusk, and several company commanders, he walked to the crest to observe the goings-on.
A panorama unfolded before them as they crested the ridge
north of Arnold's battery. Across the Emmitsburg Road, the
fight centering on the Bliss property continued to intensify,
the steady crackling of musketry indicating that the veterans
of the 39th were heavily engaged. Confederate skirmishers,
sheltered by a plank fence about 200 yards west of and paralleling the Emmitsburg Road, were giving them a hard time.
As MacDougall and the others watched, the men of the 39th
rushed forward in an attempt to take control of that fence,
but were driven back. General Hays was having none of that,
and he promptly galloped down the slope of the ridge, greet-
ing the "Guards" when they arrived back at the road, and
none too warmly. With their commander astride his horse,
his aide defiantly waving the divisional flag, and with small
arms fire whizzing past their heads, the 39th rallied, mounting
and pressing home another attack, driving the Confederates

from the fence.⁷ With their blood still up, they pushed on, advancing into first one, then another, and yet a third corral, then toward the apple orchard, and finally a meadow beyond. MacDougall recollected it as "the first and last time I ever saw a division commander with flag and staff on the skirmish line."⁸

After Hays returned to Cemetery Ridge, MacDougall was called upon to send two companies from the 111th to reinforce the skirmishers from the 125th and 126th New York regiments. The colonel escorted the two companies to the crest, then watched as they, along with four companies from the 4th Ohio, Carroll's Brigade, descended the ridge toward the Emmitsburg Road, the men from the 111th moving to the left of the 39th, and the four companies from the 4th Ohio to the right.⁹

Skirmishing commenced within minutes of their deployment along the Emmitsburg Road. All four regiments of Willard's "Harpers Ferry Cowards" were now engaged to some degree. Men from Mississippi blasted away from the cover of Farmer Bliss's apple orchard while MacDougall's two companies returned fire from the plank fence paralleling the western shoulder of the Emmitsburg Road.¹⁰

As Willard's skirmishers advanced westward from the crest of the ridge, Gibbon's Second Division closed on it from the east, with Brig. Gen. Alexander S. Webb's Philadelphia Brigade leading the way.

Chapter 4 | The 1st Minnesota and the 19th Maine

Less than a quarter hour after Willard's column had passed through Hummelbaugh's farm lane, the advance elements of Brig. Gen. John Gibbon's Second Division entered it. Like the men of Hays's division, Gibbon's columns had been temporarily placed east of the road in battalion of regiments, occupying the meadows belonging to Michael Fry, immediately south of the William Patterson farm. Fry's farm stretched south for 200 yards toward the more wooded property belonging to William's sister, Sarah Patterson.[1]

On their arrival at the Fry property Gibbon's regiments stacked arms and settled down to wait. Their artillery support, Battery A, 4th United States Light, commanded by Lt. Alonzo Cushing, and Battery B, 1st Rhode Island Light, commanded by 1st Lt. Thomas Frederick Brown, pulled off the road as well, stopping in column of sections with each carriage remaining hitched. Stretching themselves on the grass, infantry and artillerymen opened haversacks and began producing an astonishing selection of fresh food and drink.

No regiment in Gibbon's division was tougher or more seasoned than the 1st Minnesota, and their expertise extended to foraging very nearly as much as to the battlefield. They had purchased or bartered or begged or otherwise obtained

Brig. Gen. John Gibbon
National Archives

their full share of the fancy foods that were abundant in Maryland as they marched north. Fresh bread was passed around liberally as were ripe cherries, peaches, and apples. Warm milk flowed from canteens and thick blocks of gleaming white cheese were shared by brothers in arms. No doubt a flask or two made an appearance.

Colonel Colvill sat with them, enjoying his first decent meal in days. At the moment, Colvill was under informal arrest. On the march up through Maryland, he had allowed his boys to cross the Monocacy Creek single file on a log, rather than wading through the four-foot-deep water. Col. Charles Morgan, Hunt's Chief of Staff, arrived on the scene, saw what was going on, and grew irate, reporting the incident to Gibbon. The general had placed Colvill under arrest for wasting precious time during their forced march. Now Colvill waited impatiently for word that the pending charges had been rescinded. He knew that Brig. Gen. William Harrow, commanding Gibbon's First Brigade, had interceded on his behalf and was hoping that all charges would be dropped and the issue forgotten.

The wait in Fry's fields was cut short when repeated bugle calls of "Assembly" rang out from Hays's division to the north.

Within moments Second Division buglers were echoing the call to arms. Food not stuffed into hungry mouths vanished into the haversacks and weapons were unstacked. The men of Cushing's and Brown's batteries dressed ranks to the rear of their respective pieces. It was systematic and orderly, and within minutes Gibbon's people were ready to move out. They stood in formation for nearly forty-five minutes between the two Patterson farms north of Caldwell's division.

By the time the rear of Hays's column had reentered the Taneytown Road, Brig. Gen. Alexander Webb's Second Brigade had closed on it, leading Gibbon's division north. Webb's column was followed by Col. Norman Hall's Third Brigade, which in turn was followed by General Harrow's First Brigade. The division was actually facing north-northeast, toward Cemetery Hill and Artillery Ridge, when they dressed ranks before moving out. Before reentering Taneytown Road the entire division had faced about and, without losing parade formation, marched by regiments in battalion back toward the Taneytown Road. Now fronting Cemetery Ridge, the division moved into the road by brigades in column by the right flank. This maneuver was completed while Hays's column began ascending East Cemetery Ridge west of the road.

Chapter 5 | Gibbon Deploys

By the time Gibbon's column was under way, enemy rounds were flying over Cemetery Ridge at an increasing rate. Most of these projectiles overshot their intended targets on the west face of Cemetery Ridge, but this made them no less deadly to the troops east of the crest. Shells were exploding overhead, while many more duds and solid shot struck and skipped on the ground or buried themselves in the earth. Some of the Rebel gunners then firing from Seminary Ridge were attempting to gain the range of Cemetery Ridge by targeting the copse of trees, with many of their shells overshooting badly. Lacking sufficient ammunition for prolonged ranging fire, they were failing miserably to make adjustments. Although several of the gunners had gotten the range of the copse of trees south of Arnold, they failed to deliver an effective counter-battery punch to Union guns on the ridge or inflict significant damage on troops then moving along the crest.

As Webb's leading regiment closed on Hummelbaugh's lane, Cushing's and Brown's batteries swung around Harrow's trailing brigade and galloped forward, Battery A leading the way. Turning up the Hummelbaugh farm lane, they hurried toward the crest while Webb's column angled into the meadows following the well-defined swath cut by Hays. Passing the Hummelbaugh house and barn, Battery A turned north near the crest, rumbling past the Frey farm lane and on toward Arnold's battery. As Cushing's battery wheeled about in "Reverse Trot" to the left of Arnold, it was greeted by welcoming rounds fired from Seminary Ridge. Within moments of unlimbering, two of Cushing's men were down. Brown's Battery B fared better as it wheeled around in "Reverse Trot" one hundred yards south of Cushing south of the copse of trees. Although theirs was a weak and unsupported position they were low enough on the ridge so as not to attract the attention of Confederate gunners. No reports of casualties from that battery occurred at this time.

A crumbling stone wall separated Cushing's battery from Arnold's. Beginning east of the crest, the wall ran toward the brow, where it intersected the wall paralleling Arnold's front. It continued west past Arnold, descending the rise another 85 yards where it dropped to the base of the ridge then made a ninety-degree turn north toward the copse of trees and Brown's battery beyond. This lower wall ran the length of the ridge from the outer angle between Cushing and Arnold, past the left flank of Brown's battery, ending in a pile of rubble not far from the Brown's left gun.[1]

By now Hancock was on the crest directing activities. He personally ordered Cushing and Brown to open on Confederate batteries as Gibbon's Division closed on the crest. Within minutes, however, they were answered by nearly double their number engaging from Seminary Ridge, making the arrival of Gibbon's Second Brigade, under Brig. Gen. Alexander Webb, quite unnerving.[2] Webb's brigade ascended the ridge under a hail of counter-battery fire intended for Cushing and Brown. Quickly Webb's regiments were placed on the reverse slope to the left of Willard and told to lay down. Cushing and Arnold both stopped their fire to allow detachments from Webb's Brigade to pass through in order to clear a better field of fire. This proved fortunate for Webb, and the approaching Hall, because when the Federal cannons ceased their fire, the Confederate gunners following suit. While some men cleared the battery fronts of slashing, trash, and underbrush, others were sent to bolster Hay's skirmish line along the Emmitsburg Road, and to take possession of the copse of trees.[3]

Meanwhile, Colonel Hall led his men over the crest and down to the wall south of the copse of trees, extending his line southward until it connected with the right gun of Brown's Battery B, 100 yards from the thickets. When Confederate gunners saw the Third Brigade top the ridge they unleashed another short barrage that for the most part overshot Hall's unit, striking amidst Gibbon's First Brigade as it neared the crest.

As soon as his men were settled, Hall sent skirmishers forward. With no Union infantry deployed immediately to his left and with little cover available, his skirmishers were exposed to artillery fire from two sides as they advanced over open ground. Fortunately, however, the Confederate gunners failed to converge their fire, with most shells exploding off target or falling harmlessly to the ground. Brown's position could have been called precarious because his left flank was apparently in the air and uncovered. At that particular mo-

ment there were no Union troops between Brown's left and
the right gun of Capt. Judson Clark's 1st New Jersey Light,
Battery B, then supporting one of General Sickles's brigades
nearer Little Round Top, a distance of more than a mile.

It was about 8:00 A.M. when Brig. Gen. William Harrow's First Brigade, 1,366 strong, swung into Hummelbaugh's
trampled fields. Harrow had been ill during much of the
march, but while he had not been able to walk or even ride for
much of the five days, he was quite certain he had the energy
for this. Announcing that he was not about to "play it safe
during a fight," the 40 year-old brigadier led his men up the
gentle slope of East Cemetery Ridge. As his was the last of
Gibbon's three brigades to arrive, Harrow's men were placed
in reserve east of the wall and to the rear of Cushing's caisson
park, roughly 200 yards north of the left flank of Willard's
Third Brigade. For some unexplained reason, Webb deployed
portions of the 106th, 71st, and 72nd Pennsylvania regiments
into this gap, probably to help with the batteries to the front,
or perhaps the caisson parks. [4]

Harrow posted his brigade in regiments by battalion as
had Willard, stacking arms under the artillery barrage intended for Cushing, Brown, Arnold, Hall and Webb. Referred to
by many as "terrific and severe" it was nevertheless sporadic.
The copse of trees was only 100 yards to Harrow's front, just
over the crest, and Meade's headquarters, near the Taneytown
Road, were about 200 yards below and to his rear. [5]

The 19th Maine had led Harrow's brigade up the slope
after the 15th Massachusetts was detached and directed to

continue north on the Taneytown Road. Commanded by Col. Francis Edward Heath, a well-respected and gracious officer, the 543 soldiers of the 19th Maine were a no-nonsense bunch of north woodsmen, small farmers, tradesmen, fishermen, and college students.[6] Although their regiment was not yet one year old, it had participated in two major battles—Fredericksburg and Chancellorsville—and numerous smaller skirmishes. One incident in particular had stuck with Heath. On June 24, 1863, near Haymarket, Virginia, Pvt. Israel D. Jones of Company F was killed by shrapnel while the 19th was detached as Hancock's rear guard. Unable to respond to J. E. B. Stuart's horse battery that had fired the round, Colonel Heath called on his musicians to play a tune, ordered the flags unfurled, and had his men double-time out of range, carrying Jones's body with them.[7] This moment of defiance was short-lived, however, and Jones's bloody corpse was unceremoniously buried in a shallow grave alongside the pike. His burial haunted Heath his entire life. Of all his Civil War actions, Heath most regretted not having made time for a proper Christian burial. Sometimes one casualty can be more painful than a dozen.[8]

Heath was directed to

Colonel Francis E. Heath
Maine State Archives,
Augusta, Me.

place his regiment on the reverse slope of the ridge, east of and below Cushing's caissons, near an extension of the wall that separated the 126th New York from Arnold's caisson park, and the 106th Pennsylvania, from both batteries. Shot and shell intended for Cushing passed overhead, some of it landing squarely on Heath's position. The real killer, shrapnel, exploded 10–20 feet above the ground, sending jagged chunks of hot lead and iron shot earthward over a hundred-foot-square area.[9] For the soldiers hugging the earth it was a trying time. Sgt. Silas Adams described it:

> The Confederate made no attack in front of the position we were holding in the forenoon, but they evidently knew we were there. Every now and then they would pitch a shell over among us, which would strike in our midst, killing and wounding a number of men. All we could do was lie there and guess where the next one would strike, or whom the next victim would be. We were near enough to the crest of the hill [ridge] to get the full benefit of their fireworks.[10]

Heath lost only one man killed and 12 wounded, one mortally, from this shelling. Farther east, below the crest, two more regiments were ordered to lie down. They too took light casualties from this fire. One of these regiments was the 82nd New York. The other was the 1st Minnesota.

Chapter 6 | Enter the 1st Minnesota

Col. William Colvill's 1st Minnesota stacked arms several rods to the rear of Heath's 19th Maine. Two hundred yards to the north, just this side of Bryan's peach orchard, Colvill could see the stacked arms of the 111th New York and, a little nearer, those of the 71st Pennsylvania. The colonel's 329 men and officers completed stacking their arms while the 15th Massachusetts, moving at double-quick to their left, crested the ridge near the copse of trees. After being detached, the 15th had continued north on the Taneytown Road, then ascended the ridge using the rural lane belonging to Peter Frey.[1] After dropping their personal items, they continued up and over the crest, passing to the left of Cushing's caisson park and battery.

A bugle sounded assembly, calling the 82nd New York to their feet. Colvill's veterans paid little attention as the 82nd reformed and dressed. Within moments of the first bugle call the New Yorkers were winding their way west, through the ranks of the 1st Minnesota and then 19th Maine. Turning left at the stone wall, they passed to the rear of Cushing caissons, then west again, following the 15th over the crest. Continuing across the "Broad Open Plain" to the Emmitsburg Road, the 15th and 82nd formed a skirmish line that extended from the left of the 39th New York south toward the Codori farm.

With the 15th and 82nd detached, Harrow was down to two regiments mustering 769 effectives. Webb had even fewer effectives with less than 700 men between his two remaining regiments, the 71st and 72nd Pennsylvania. In all, Gibbon's Second Division had roughly 1,410 men in reserve.[2]

With the activity passed, some of Colvill's veterans again opened haversacks and returned to their partially eaten meals. Others rested, read letters, or chatted about home. While marching through Maryland, the rumors had started that they were moving toward the battles of all battles, but thus far all that had happened was a lot of marching and another change in the Army of the Potomac's commanding officer. Hooker was out. There was a hot rumor that Maj. Gen. George B. McClellan would take over but as it turned out, Maj. Gen. George G. Meade was the new commander. The men expected that there would be some reorganization and maybe, eventually, some fighting, but for the time being at least, they anticipated nothing like the recent fight at Chancellorsville.

Colonel Colvill's regiment was comprised of 29 officers and about 300 effectives using .58 caliber Sharps Rifles and .69 caliber smoothbores, an unusual but lethal pairing, particularly at close range.[3] For now, however, these arms remained stacked on the eastern brow of Cemetery Ridge within sight of the copse of trees. Like the 19th Maine above them, the 1st Minnesota suffered under a sporadic but sometimes lethal barrage for roughly four hours, unable to respond or protect themselves. Despite the noise and the stress, the rising heat and the occasional artillery shell, many of the men nodded off to sleep.[4]

The 1st Minnesota was the first regiment offered to the Federal government for an extended period of service, mustered in on April 29, 1861. No unit with the Army of the Potomac had seen more combat service than these frontiersmen from the northwest, and their reputa-

Brig. Gen. John C. Caldwell
National Archives

tion extended throughout the army. Their leader, a 33-year-old lawyer turned journalist, had mustered in with the regiment as a Brevet Captain in command of Company F. William Colvill was as rough as his northern Red-Wings and, at 6'5," he towered over most of them. Unlike many volunteer officers who disdained the company of enlisted personnel, Colvill relished it, and he demanded no more of his enlisted men than he did of himself or his junior officers.

Within 15 minutes of Harrow's brigade vacating Hummelbaugh's intersection, Brig. Gen. John Caldwell's First Division entered it. Like Hays and Gibbon before him, Caldwell had temporarily placed his men east of the Taneytown Road. Unlike the other two divisions, however, who were placed in fairly open meadows, Caldwell's division took cover in a belt of woods belonging to Sarah Patterson, just north of Blacksmith Shop Road.[5] Their stay was short. The column returned to the road at about 8:00 A.M., just as Gibbon's Second

Division was moving through the intersection. The forward elements of Caldwell's First Division began passing through the intersection at about 8:45 A.M. but, instead of following the trampled path left by Hays and Gibbon, the division marched by the left flank directly up the slope, advancing through the Hummelbaugh and Peter Frey farms. Lt. Albert Sheldon's 1st New York Battery B, 14th Independent attached, rumbled up Cemetery Ridge using Hummelbaugh's farm lane. As the division advanced over a broad front, Sheldon led his battery north on the reverse slope below the crest, passing near the Hummelbaugh barn, then in use as General Tyler's Reserve Artillery headquarters.

At this juncture, Meade and Hancock still assumed that General Humphreys's division, Sickles's Third Corps, would deploy back to the ridge south of the Hummelbaugh Farm lane and connect with Caldwell's left to the north. Birney would redeploy northward to connect with Humphreys's left as soon as the Fifth Corps arrived to relieve Birney near the Little Round Top. With this in mind, Caldwell's massed brigades ascended the ridge by battalion, their right flank a hundred yards or so south of Gibbon's reserve regiments, the 1st Minnesota and 19th Maine, their left flank nearer the Hummelbaugh farm lane, covering a front of about 400 yards overall. Sheldon's guns remained hitched to the front in anticipation of rapid deployment.

Most of Caldwell's men stacked arms and lay down, although not all of his men were so lucky. Several detachments from each regiment were sent forward to dismantle rail and plank fences, standing between Cemetery Ridge and the Emmitsburg Road, most of which belonged to farmer Nicholas Codori. The crest of Cemetery Ridge was open and about 100 yards wide above where Caldwell massed his division, which was why he chose to stay on the opposite slope. Had his command crested the ridge there would have been no good ground to secure and his men would have been subjected to artillery fire on that open crest. Even then, a few rounds fired from across the valley found their mark within the ranks. Rather than respond to this sporadic shelling, Caldwell ordered Lieutenant Sheldon to keep his four 10-pounders concealed east of the crest, knowing that to expose the battery would bring on far more intense artillery fire than they were then experiencing.[6] Sheldon's four Parrot Rifles were parked to the front of the center of Caldwell's division,[7] approximately 150 yards north-northwest of Hummelbaugh's barn.[8]

Chapter 7 | The Growing Crisis on the Left

It was about this time that Hancock became genuinely concerned about the Second Corps' left flank. Humphreys had not taken his expected position on the ridge south of Caldwell and there were no indications he would do so anytime soon. As a result, Caldwell's left flank was completely exposed. One of Hancock's aides was dispatched to army headquarters to inform General Meade of the situation, at which point the army commander sent several couriers to General Sickles instructing him to correct the problem and adhere to general orders. Instead of complying with Meade's request to move Humphreys back to the ridge, Sickles opted to send back notes describing the high ground to Humphreys's front—the Emmitsburg Road Rise. Sickles did not like the position assigned to his Corps, and had no intention of occupying it.

Humphreys's position had become a real problem for everyone. He had not yet established his line, and what there was of it appeared too far forward and too low. To allow him to move even farther west, to the Emmitsburg Road, would isolate him further, placing his line out of touch with the Second Corps and the rest of the army. The arrival of Col. George C. Burling's 1,600 effectives might have helped to improve the situation had general orders been followed, but instead,

Humphreys placed the newly arrived brigade west of Plum Run, just east of and below the Klingle house. Humphreys did this with full knowledge of the situation and general orders. He was well aware that his right wing was supposed to connect with Caldwell's left. This last move infuriated Hancock, who reportedly sent Meade another message suggesting that Sickles was not going to comply.

The skirmishing along Hancock's front continued to escalate, and by 10:00 A.M. had developed into a very nasty fight, particularly around the William Bliss farm.[1] From right to left, the batteries of Woodruff, Arnold, Cushing, and Brown all opened in support of Hays as his division continued their attempts to drive the Rebels out. The skirmishing continued to intensify until a major counter-charge by portions of Hays's division finally alerted army headquarters that another front had developed west of the Baltimore Pike. Still, little was done to remedy the Sickles situation. If a full Confederate attack had commenced at that moment, there was no way Humphreys's people could have held their position. Both his flanks were wide open to direct enfilade. The angle of the low ground on which his division rested placed his men with their backs at a slight left-oblique to Caldwell's west-facing line. Rather than linking up with the Second Corps, he had moved away and turned his back on it. In so doing, Humphreys not only placed himself in jeopardy, but also Caldwell and the entire Second Corps.

To add to the worsening situation, General Birney had allowed Ward to move his brigade away from South Cemetery Ridge and Little Round Top to a lesser rise west of Plum Run.[2] Brig. Gen. Charles K. Graham's First Brigade was detached even farther west, taking up position on the reverse, or east, slope of the Emmitsburg Road Rise east of the Sherfy farm. Birney's two supporting batteries, previously positioned at the base of the ridge near the Wheatfield Road, had disappeared too, and were now sitting idle near the Trostle farm.[3] Birney had also let Col. Regis De Trobriand's newly arrived Third Brigade stack arms north of the Stony Hill near Col. George C. Burling's brigade, which by now had been detached from Humphreys's Second Division. No effort was made to pull any of these brigades back toward the low ridge or small round-topped mountain on the left. Despite Sickles's professed interest in the high ground to his front, he had placed most of his artillery brigade in the low ground along Plum Run nearer Humphrey's two remaining brigades. From the mountain on the left, north to the Hummelbaugh's farm lane, a distance of over one mile, Cemetery Ridge was basically devoid of Federal troops.

By 11:30 A.M. it was evident that Caldwell's division had become the left flank of the Army of the Potomac then occupying Cemetery Ridge. As message after message was passed along time ticked away. Sickles's intentions became very apparent when, near noon, De Trobriand's brigade could be seen moving south-southeast toward the Wheatfield, with Graham advancing toward the Emmitsburg Road. During a forenoon meeting at army headquarters the Sickles dilemma was discussed. Sickles, a no-show, would arrive moments after the meeting and after Hancock had left. Meade, meanwhile, suggested to Hancock that he take whatever measures he could to correct the damage. The first thing Hancock did was turn to General Hunt and request artillery support. Hunt obliged by turning to General Tyler and requesting that Ransom's Regulars be sent to Cemetery Ridge. Finally, Hunt was instructed to ride over to the left and see what the hell Sickles was up to.[4]

With the meeting long ended, Hancock, accompanied by Col. Charles Morgan, the Second Corps' inspector-general and his chief of staff, rode south, passing the Peter Frey house. He found Caldwell somewhere near the Hummelbaugh farm lane.[5] The three officers rode to the crest of the ridge, where they dismounted. Hancock pointed due south, toward the stone house belonging to George Weikert, telling Caldwell to take his entire division down yonder, including Battery B. Caldwell nodded, then left to put in motion the orders that would transport his entire division nearly one-half-mile south.[6]

Chapter 8 | Weir and Thomas: Two Batteries Arrive

Leaving Caldwell to his duties, Hancock turned back north in time to see two regular batteries cresting the ridge south of the copse of trees. These were the two batteries Hunt had promised. The first was Battery C, 4th United States Light Artillery, commanded by 19-year-old Lt. Evan Thomas, son of Gen. Lorenzo Thomas, Adjutant General of the United States Army. The other was Battery C, 5th United States Light Artillery, commanded by 25-year-old Lt. Gulian Verplanck Weir, son of Professor Robert Weir, Head Instructor of Drawing, United States Military Academy at West Point. Although both officers were young, they were already seasoned veterans of many battles, and their efforts had received favorable comment from senior officers.[1]

Hancock spurred his horse toward the approaching column, waving it to a halt. In the narrow farm lane that paralleled the crest, the general was joined by Gibbon. Lieutenant Thomas explained that he and Weir had been ordered to report to the Second Corps. Hancock ordered Gibbon to place Weir's battery where he saw fit, then told Thomas to follow him. Hancock led Thomas southward, down the western slope toward Plum Run and into a rock-strewn field near some uneven and stony ground at the base of the ridge. Just north of this low rough ground the Codori and Hummelbaugh farm lanes intersected. This east-west artery was a much-traveled short cut connecting the Emmitsburg and Taneytown Roads. It would soon become critical to Meade's entire position, and the rural connecting crossroads had to be held at all costs. If not, the Confederates would have a direct route into the rear of the Army of the Potomac. Hancock ordered the battery to halt. Meanwhile, Caldwell's pioneers were busily removing rails from the fences lining the two farm lanes.

At first sight, Thomas's position appeared a terrible place, with Plum Run but 100 yards away. The brush and thickets along its banks were higher than a mounted officer, not that this mattered as the rise beyond Plum Run blocked most of Thomas's view to the west anyway. The meadow to his left was open as it descended toward Plum Run, then gradually rose before the ridge fell away to the south, beyond a dry ravine and grassy knoll 300 yards distant. The knoll extended west, beyond Thomas's gun line, and blocked any view of Trostle's meadows west of the run. Due south, Thomas could see large trees surrounding George Weikert's stone house, and perhaps the roof, but not the house itself. Certainly he never mentioned it. He did, however, have an unobstructed view of the meadow as it descended toward the ravine where it intersected Plum Run. To the west-northwest, he could see all the way to the Codori buildings and beyond, to the Bliss farm. To his front he could see the Rogers farm and Seminary Ridge beyond. His view, therefore, was a commanding one, save to his left-center, west of the run, where the rise and knoll blocked everything.[2]

If enemy riflemen gained either that rise, or the knoll beyond the dry ravine off his left flank, they could shoot into his gun line from 200 yards away. If both rises were occupied, Thomas's position would become untenable. To his immediate right low rough ground formed a natural amphitheater at the base of the ridge. A low elongated rise, whose southernmost part housed Thomas right section, wound through the rough ground paralleling the run. A scattering of small trees and brush offered some slight protection. Beyond the low marshy rough ground, Plum Run flowed through Codori's meadows from the Emmitsburg Road, 900 yards distant. Thomas's position was so low that he couldn't see over the Emmitsburg Road as it angled past his front. Looking back toward Cemetery Hill, all he could see were North Cemetery Ridge, a portion of the copse of trees, and the top of Ziegler's Grove.[3]

Hancock told Thomas that Third Corps units were beyond the rise west of Plum Run. If they moved back to Cemetery Ridge as he expected they would connect with the battery's left flank. The general told Thomas to hold his fire and to keep his caissons parked out of sight, whereupon the nineteen-year-old lieutenant, perhaps impertinently, requested that infantry be sent to support this seemingly isolated position. Thomas had a point and Hancock readily agreed with it. Caldwell's people would be of no use where they were headed and Hancock decided to send one or more units to support young Thomas, a decision that was sound both tactically and politically. Only a fool would leave the son of the adjutant general of the United States Army in an isolated pocket to be overrun, and Hancock was no fool.

Meanwhile, Gibbon had parked Weir's six 12-pounder Napoleons on the reverse slope south of the 1st Minnesota, near where the departing Sheldon's 1st New York, Battery B had been parked. This was done as Caldwell's division crossed over Hummelbaugh's farm lane, moving by the left flank. It would come as a surprise to Hunt that neither Thomas nor Weir accompanied Caldwell, a fact he would discover later that day. Hunt did not notice Thomas's position until after the fight had begun, at which time he thought the battery vulnerable.[4]

Caldwell's left-flank march was completed without incident as his division moved nearly one–half mile south, staying below the crest on the reverse slope of Cemetery Ridge. His division again went into position in columns of regiments by brigades with the 1st New York Battery B assuming its position in the front-center. This time, however, Lieutenant Sheldon's four Parrotts were unhitched and rolled to the crest. Because of the knoll between his position and Thomas's Battery C, Lieutenant Sheldon probably could not see Thomas's guns, although he may well have seen Thomas's caissons on the west brow of the ridge. For his part, although Thomas knew Caldwell had moved, it is doubtful that he witnessed it or that he could see the First Division or Battery B.[5] At that moment, he must have felt very much alone.

Chapter 9 | The 19th Maine and 1st Minnesota Move Forward

O n his way back toward the copse of trees, Hancock again encountered Gibbon. They discussed the situation as 1:00 P.M. came and went. Hancock told Gibbon to be prepared to send two regiments to Humphreys and the Third Corps if and when they were needed. He also directed Gibbon to send a regiment to support Lieutenant Thomas's Battery C and bring yet another forward to bolster the line south of the copse of trees. For his part, Gibbon told Hancock where he had placed Weir's battery. Hancock then disappeared over the crest of the ridge in search of General Meade. By 2:00 P.M. small arms fire from beyond the Emmitsburg Road had escalated into a major skirmish with powder smoke now rising beyond the tree line on South Seminary Ridge. Sickles's Third Corps was engaged.[1]

After consulting with the Brigadier General Harrow, Gibbon sent orders to Colonel Heath, instructing him to bring the 19th Maine forward. Heath's regiment was conducted over the crest and placed in line to the rear of the tumbled-down stone wall south of Brown's Rhode Islanders and the copse of trees.[2] Meanwhile, Colonel Colvill was instructed to take the 1st Minnesota south to support Thomas's Battery C.[3] With Caldwell's division gone and with Colvill's regiment headed south, the 19th's left flank was in the air.[4] Despite being in the very middle of the Union line on Cemetery Ridge, this unit had become, in the words of one of its members, "particularly alone on that ... part of the field." [5]

As Colvill and Heath were moving their regiments to their new positions, Meade galloped by on his way to see Sickles. Hunt had returned to headquarters to inform Meade that Sickles was engaged far to the front and that he doubted Sickles was going to comply with general orders. Meade was livid, and set out to reposition Sickles's troops, this time in person. As he approached Trostle's Lane, Meade spotted a massed column of blue emerging from the low ground of Trostle's meadows heading south-southeast toward Little Round Top. This was Humphreys's division. Perhaps Hunt, who had spoken with Sickles, had indeed persuaded him to do something. Whatever the case, Meade found Sickles east of Plum Run watching Humphreys's division march south. While they conferred, Hunt approached from the direction of the ridge. As the three generals conversed, a distant boom turned all eyes toward the Emmitsburg Road Rise. Longstreet's Artillery had opened the ball.

It was nearly 3:00 P.M. when Meade told Sickles that the enemy would probably not allow him to pull back to conform to the rest of the line and that he was on his own until help arrived from the Fifth Corps. The irate Meade spun his horse around while telling Sickles he would see what he could do. Meanwhile Hunt, accompanied by Colonel Warner, rode off in another direction. Disregarding the security of Cemetery Ridge in favor of strengthening Sickles's Third Corps' artillery deployment, he would call for reinforcements from Tyler's Artillery Reserves, siphoning off all but a few guns and leaving no reserves available for Hancock. This breach would spark a feud between Hunt and Hancock that would culminate on the morrow and continue for many years.

Meanwhile, Hancock had returned to Cemetery Ridge in time to watch Humphreys's entire division, flags streaming and bands playing, reverse their line of march from south-southeast to west-northwest, away from the ridge and back toward Trostle's meadows. Someone commented on how splendid they looked and Hancock, in his acid way, remarked, "watch them, they'll come tumbling back, soon enough." At about this moment, Meade stopped on his return to headquarters to converse briefly with Hancock, then sped over the ridge toward his headquarters at the Leister house.

After their conversation, Hancock remounted and galloped south along the ridge, passing the 19th Maine, Battery C, and the relocated 1st Minnesota, until he found Caldwell and ordered him to take his division to support Sickles. He countermanded this order immediately, however, when he saw units belonging to Brig. Gen. James Barnes's First Division, Fifth Corps, heading west across Cemetery Ridge, north of Little Round Top. Caldwell's division immediately reversed its march and returned to its second position on Cemetery Ridge north of the George Weikert homestead.[76]

By this time the sky was full of exploding projectiles and missiles. The Peach Orchard was shrouded in black powder smoke as several volunteer reserve batteries destined for Sickles's front rumbled by the 1st Minnesota, passing behind where they now lay. Below Colvill, Thomas's men relaxed near their assigned position, many passing the time napping. North and west of them, the fight for the Bliss property that had died away was heating up again, with unrelenting skirmishing and heavy casualties. Hazard's three right batteries, from left to right, Cushing, Arnold, and Woodruff, having received direct orders from Hancock, were once again engaged in both counter-battery and infantry fire.

Hancock's center would just have to make do with less—Meade again instructed him to send support to the left. The first thing Hancock did was direct Gibbon to send in the two regiments they had discussed earlier. Gibbon called on the 19th Massachusetts and 42nd New York. Pulling them out of Hall's line left a huge gap in the Second Corps between the right of the 19th Maine and the left of 20th Massachusetts, the latter just north of the copse of trees. To cover this gap Gibbon sent word to Lieutenant Brown to shift his Rhode Island Battery forward and to the right, in front of the stone wall west of the copse of trees. He then brought up the 71st and 72nd Pennsylvania to bolster the 106th Pennsylvania near the copse of trees. This left Willard's "Harpers Ferry Cowards" as the only viable reserve unit in the Union center.

Brown's six guns were hastened forward and placed in battery in front of some rocky rough ground 60 yards west of the copse of trees. This move meant that the nearest unit to the 19th Maine was Weir's 5th U.S. Battery C, still parked in reserve east of the crest and 300 yards southeast of Heath's left flank. Farther to the left, beyond the Hummelbaugh farm lane near the western base of the ridge, were the six guns of Thomas's 4th U.S. East of Thomas lay the 1st Minnesota. Thomas's battery and Colvill's regiment were the only organized units then defending the center of the Union line between Heath's 19th Maine and Caldwell's division, a distance of nearly half a mile.

By this time the battle was raging as far south as the eye could see. Longstreet's legions were sweeping eastward, pressing all before them. Desperate Union troops fought to hold crumbling positions on Little Round Top, Houck's Ridge, Rose Woods, the Wheatfield, Stony Hill, and all along the Emmitsburg Road. General Tyler was feeding reserve battery after reserve battery over Cemetery Ridge to Sickles's front, most of them bypassing the Hummelbaugh farm lane for the George Weikert lane, which cut through Patterson's Woods near Caldwell's left flank. Had these batteries used Hummelbaugh's Lane, it is almost certain Hancock or Gibbon would have commandeered several.[7]

Again Hancock rode south to meet with Caldwell. After conversing with the general, he stayed while Father William Corby gave the Irish Brigade general absolution. Hancock noted that Sheldon's 1st New York, Battery B, did not accompany Caldwell when his division again started south. He would remember this battery and in short order would, although unknowingly, add fuel to a kindling that would ignite into a fire between him and Hunt on July Third.

It was nearing 5:00 P.M. when Hancock again returned north, stopping en route to speak with Lieutenant Thomas. The general's exact route is unknown. He may or may not have seen the 1st Minnesota, but if he did, he made no mention of it. All the same, it is more than likely he was aware of its presence, as this was the fourth time he had passed them since that regiment had moved.

Chapter 10 | Turnbull's Battery

After leaving Thomas, Hancock was riding north on the ridge when Lt. John Turnbull's 3rd United States Artillery, Consolidated Batteries F and K, of Ransom's Regular Reserves, bounded over the crest headed toward the Emmitsburg Road. Turnbull's battery was followed by Weir's six Napoleons, which were supposed to have been detached to Hancock to begin with. Both Turnbull and Weir had received orders from General Tyler to proceed to the aid of General Humphreys's division. Again, everything was being sacrificed to support Sickles. Although Turnbull got past Hancock, Weir was not so lucky. Halted by the general for the second time that afternoon, the lieutenant was asked what his orders were. Weir responded that he had been instructed to report to the Emmitsburg Road.

One glance told Hancock this would not do. The raging battle was obscured by smoke and dust, but Sickles's masses retreating north and east told the story. They were tumbling back just as Hancock had predicted. Sickles's salient at the Peach Orchard had already collapsed and Longstreet's attack was rapidly moving north, up the Emmitsburg Road.

Not wanting to get caught in Codori's narrow fence-lined farm lane, Turnbull passed over Plum Run north of it, rumbling toward the Emmitsburg Road at a gallop, his cannoneers mounted on the chests, holding on for dear life. Turnbull reported personally to General Humphreys, who directed him to a position just south of Peter Rogers's small white clapboard home, near where the Emmitsburg Road angled due north. Men from the 11th and 16th Massachusetts Infantry regiments helped tear down the plank fence on either side of the road to allow his passage. Turnbull unlimbered just south of Rogers's pleasant little yard, a freshly painted white picket fence very near the lieutenant's right gun. Humphreys pointed to a Confederate battery some 1,200 yards away.[1] "Silence them," he said.

Before Turnbull could comply, however, he was hailed from afar by an approaching horseman, coming at full gallop. It was Captain Ransom. The captain had returned to his headquarters near Hummelbaugh's barn to find his brigade dispersed and, accompanied by 1st Lt. Henry Christiancy, one of Humphreys's aides, he had set out to find his batteries. Turnbull relayed Humphreys's orders to Ransom, who then rode forward to reconnoiter as the lieutenant was bringing his guns to bear.

Ransom was riding into a hornet's nest. The captain descended into a wide swale and rode up the next rise, its crest occupied by nine companies of Col. Clark Baldwin's 1st Massachusetts Infantry, who had been skirmishing with Confederates in this area for over an hour. Their position was strung out along the fairly open crest of the rise, the men having taken cover behind a stout rail fence. Another crest, about three hundred yards west of this one, was swarming with Confederates and the mounted officer made an inviting target. Within moments a minie ball thudded into Ransom's right thigh six inches above the knee. Despite the wound, the captain remained on his now-skittish horse and quickly descended back into the swale. As he galloped east, bullets whipped by him, grazing his horse and even clipping its tail.[2]

Weir and Hancock could see that Turnbull had already come under fire as he swung his battery about at "Reverse Trot." Looking south down the ridge toward the 1st Minnesota and beyond, where Caldwell had been, Hancock could see the whole situation unfolding before him. He decided at that moment that he would hold that portion of the ridge at all costs. Weir later recalled to Hunt:

> Gen. Hancock stopped me near the crest demanding my orders. I told him I had instructions to report to Gen Humphreys and was to accompany Lt. Turnbull. I had received these orders from Captain [Lt. Gustav von Blucher] Blocker, acting aide-de-camp Artillery Reserve. I presumed they had come from yourself or Gen Tyler.[3]

From where they sat their horses, Weir and Hancock could see the Rogers house quite clearly and the skirmish lines blazing away beyond it. Turnbull was already fully engaged, less than 50 yards south of the white picket fence, supported by portions of Brig. Gen. Joseph Carr's Third Brigade. Carr's men were the end of Sickles's line, anchoring his far right flank.

It was a little after 5:00 P.M. when Hancock again led

Weir north, possibly to replace Brown's Rhode Island Battery off Colonel Heath's left flank. Hancock was aware of the 300-yard wide gap that had been opened when Brown's battery was moved forward and it bothered him. Weir reported, "About 4:00-o'clock [actually much later] I was ordered by Major-General Hancock to take up a position about 500 yards to the right and front [of Hummelbaugh lane], with orders to watch my front, as our troops were falling back on the left at the same time."[4]

As Hancock led Weir north, they encountered Meade, accompanied by Gibbon, approaching from the opposite direction. While Hancock and Meade conversed, General Gibbon sent an aide to Weir, instructing the lieutenant to unlimber his battery on the crest where it had stopped. Unknown to Weir, Meade had placed Hancock in command of the Third Corps and Gibbon in command of the Second after Sickles was seriously wounded by a Confederate artillery shot.[5] Because Weir's guns would undoubtedly draw counter-battery fire, Gibbon did not want his gun line too close to the infantry. The guns were unlimbered on the crest 200 yards southeast of the 19th Maine, north of Hummelbaugh's farm lane. The gap between the 19th Maine and the copse of trees remained open.

When the conversation of the generals broke up, Gibbon rode back to Weir, and ordered him to open with solid shot to establish the range, following with case at four-degree elevation. Weir's gunners targeted a Confederate line of infantry emerging onto the broad open plain from the canopy of woods atop South Seminary Ridge, probably the brigades belonging to Brig. Gen. Cadmus Wilcox and Col. David Lang. Weir's gunners and artillerists worked feverishly on the exposed crest. At the peak of the afternoon, with the guns roaring and burning to the touch and the smoke eddying around them, it was blisteringly hot. Oddly, there was no counter-battery fire from Seminary Ridge, or if there was, Weir never reported it.[6]

By this time the entire Union Line along the Emmitsburg Road south of Trostle's lane was in shambles. The Stony Hill and Houck's Ridge were in enemy hands as were most of the Wheatfield and Trostle's Woods. The Confederates were driving steadily through the Peach Orchard where once-stiff resistance had crumbled. Caldwell's division had pressed home an energetic attack through the Wheatfield and Rose Woods, but was flanked and shot to pieces. Forced back, the survivors retired north of the Wheatfield Road. They would be pushed back even further. From as far north as the copse of trees, Colonel Willard and staff, watching from the crest, could feel Longstreet's assault rolling up the Emmitsburg Road toward them as much as they could see it. The valley was in chaos and what they could see were flashes and

Col. David Lang
Valentine Museum, Richmond, Va.

shapes and men and horses moving in the smoke. They knew it was going very badly. Already hundreds of retreating and disorganized troops could be seen milling about on the slopes of Cemetery Ridge just south of Weir's battery.

From near the spot where he had conversed with Meade, Hancock was doing his best to address the developing problem. First, he sent an aide north to instruct General Hays to send a brigade to the left, directing it to guide on Sheldon's 1st New York, Battery B, which Hancock thought was in Caldwell's former position. Finding Hays in conversation with Colonel Willard, Hancock's aide saluted and excused himself, then stated, "General Hancock sends his compliments and wishes you to send one of your brigades over there," all the while pointing south toward Sheldon's supposed position.[7]

It has been said that the aide told Hays to have whomever he sent report to General Birney, but this is most unlikely. Hancock wanted the brigade where Caldwell had been. When Caldwell's division moved south, it left a yawning gap in the line. Hancock needed someone—anyone—to fill that gap. Hancock also sent couriers hustling to get help from Generals Baxter and Doubleday of the First Corps, and to inform Meade of the developing crisis. He sent riders galloping off to the Eleventh and Twelfth Corps, and to the Artillery Reserve Park. This last courier would find the park nearly empty, because Hunt had already commandeered most of the guns to help Sickles. It was nearing 5:30 P.M.[8]

By this time, Humphreys's division was fully engaged, its left wing having already changed direction, forming a salient fronting south and west. Lt. Gen. Ambrose P. Hill's Third Army Corps joined the attack as General Wilcox's Alabamans went in off Longstreet's left, north of Brig. Gen. William Barksdale's Mississippi Brigade. Hunt's reserve batteries regrouped around the Trostle farm and east of Plum Run in a desperate attempt to stem the rising Confederate tide. They were too little and too late. The guns could not hold the Peach Orchard line and as the position collapsed in total panic, a Chancellorsville-type rout seemed in the offing. If the Confederate advance was to be stopped it had fallen on Hancock to do it.

Chapter 11 | Hancock's Reinforcements

Willard was standing next to General Hays when Hancock's call for reinforcements arrived. "Take your brigade over there and knock the hell out of them," Hays said to Willard, and Willard barked the order to fall in.[1] Save for portions of the 39th New York, many having returned east of the road, and smaller detachments from the 111th, 125th, and 126th New York, who were still skirmishing at the Bliss farm, most of Colonel Willard's "Harpers Ferry Cowards," had spent the last several hours lying down east of the crest. The tension for the men under Willard's command broke as orders ran down the line and they cheered as they fell in and dressed ranks. Within seconds rifles were un-stacked and everything save bayonets, ammunition, caps, and canteens was cast aside. No haversacks, no wool blankets, no shelter–halves. If there had been shirkers before, there were none this time. No one volunteered to guard the piles of personal belongings left behind as the men dressed ranks.

Willard led his column forward at the double-quick, passing the stacked piles of accoutrements left by the 71st and 72nd Pennsylvania, the 1st Minnesota and the 19th Maine. Snaking their way along the reverse slope of the ridge, they continued past Cushing's caissons, the copse of trees, and

Webb's brigade to their right, and the Peter Frey farm below to the left. Case and shrapnel passed overhead or exploded just yards away. Percussion shells intended for the crest pock-marked the wide eastern slope, several crashing into Frey's large gray stone house. Solid shot and bolt bounded and whirred about them as the "Harpers Ferry Cowards" passed beyond Weir's battery limbering on the crest. Continuing past the Hummelbaugh farmyard, the site of a field hospital now littered with wounded, dead, and piles of amputated limbs, they crossed over the farm lane.

Once south of the lane the brigade began encountering Second, Third, and even Fifth Corps survivors from the Union left. To the right, the Emmitsburg Road was roiling in smoke and flame as Carr's right wing desperately tried to hold its flanked position. Hancock's entire front was ablaze with roll-ing musketry punctuated with the boom of cannon. Thomas's battery stood at the ready as Willard's men moved past. To Thomas's front, out near the road, Turnbull was hitching his guns at fixed prolonge[2] in what would become the bloodiest and longest supporting withdrawal of any battery that day. "Retire while firing," Carr had told him. A flat-out skeddadle was not only undignified—it could create a panic, and pos-sible catastrophe for the Army of the Potomac.

Willard passed Thomas's battery, and then the 1st Min-nesota. Continuing south an additional 500 odd–yards, the "Harpers Ferry Cowards" passed through increasing numbers of Federals returning from the south, including many from Caldwell's First Division. Colonel Willard brought his brigade to a halt near where Lieutenant Sheldon's 1st New York, Battery B, had been positioned only a few minutes earlier. Commandeered by Col. Edward Warner, Battery B had been rushed 400 yards further south to cover Trostle's Farm Lane from a point nearer the George Weikert House.[3]

Willard formed his line of battle on the crest of the ridge with Patterson's woods 200 yards to his rear. A few retreating troops faced about and joined his fresh ranks, but for the most part they swarmed past, through, or rallied around the regiments in small groups. Ambulances, some loaded with wounded and dying men, were being hauled along the ridge, as were caissons, and supporting wagons, all adding to the mass of confusion. Walking wounded and litter-bearers made for Patterson's woods while the slope to the brigade's front swarmed with retreating troops. The colonel took his position, mounted to the front of his command; and waited.

To Willard's left along Trostle's lane, unnoticed in the confusion but soon to play an important role along with the 39th New York, Col. Freeman McGilvery, commander of Tyler's First Volunteer Brigade, Reserve Artillery, was placing guns in line as quickly they appeared. Among those guns was Sheldon's 1st New York, Battery B. McGilvery

Lt. Col. Freeman McGilvery
National Archives

had already placed Lt. Malbone Watson's 5th U.S. Battery I, just south of Trostle's lane above Plum Run, possibly sacrificing that command in order to buy time. Sheldon was next in line 400 yards east of Watson.

Colonels William R. Brewster and De Trobriand attempted to rally fleeing troops between Willard's right and the 1st Minnesota's left. This gap of over 500 yards now imperiled the Army of the Potomac's entire position. If it was breeched Meade would not only lose the Taneytown Road, his vital line of supply, but his army would be split. Three hundred yards south of Willard, where the rural farm lane paralleling the ridge intersected Trostle's lane, the Taneytown Road could be reached through a connecting lane via Patterson's Woods. This vital intersection had to be held. Caldwell was rallying troops near this intersection and Sheldon's battery, with some success. These Second and Third Corps fugitives pitched in with the right of the Fifth Corps to hold their position south and west of George Weikert's embattled farm, but still the Confederate line pressed forward.

Hancock desperately needed to buy time. It would be a quarter-hour, perhaps longer, before any of the reinforcements he requested could arrive from the east. At this time he had with him his personal aide, Capt. William Miller, and his color-bearer, Pvt. James Wells. All the rest of his aides had been dispatched elsewhere. Hancock could see Humphreys's line crumbling south of the Klingle house. He galloped back toward Weir's 5th U.S. battery. Riding up to Weir, he demanded that the lieutenant follow him. The battery limbered just as

Willard's brigade moved past its rear. Hancock led Weir forward, dropping off the crest of the ridge due east of the Codori farm and out onto the broad open plain. Rumbling over the same route Turnbull had taken, north of Codori's farm lane, Hancock directed Battery C into position about 300 yards east-southeast of Codori's large red barn. Weir could see that Lieutenant Turnbull was at fixed prolonge, slowly retiring his six Napoleons eastward, keeping pace with Carr's back–tracking right flank. Looking toward the Codori barn and the battle blazing around it, Weir protested.[4] How could he hold such an exposed position without infantry support?

There was no infantry available at that moment. Hancock said, "You go in here and I will bring you support." Without another word to Hancock, Weir ordered his bugler to sound "Reverse Trot." Battery C unlimbered facing west-southwest, at a slight left angle to the Emmitsburg Road, its right flank aligned with the Codori barn. Before the first gun's trail hit the ground, Hancock, Miller, and Wells were off to fetch the promised support. Weir opened with solid shot, firing over Carr's line and the retiring Turnbull. He switched to spherical case in an attempt to slow down the advancing Confederates under Wilcox and Lang.

Lieutenant Thomas could see Weir north of him, beyond Plum Run, where the creek bent toward the Emmitsburg Road. The only thing between him and Weir was fleeing Third Corps infantry. The gap between Thomas's right and the 82nd New York, who formed Gibbon's left at the Codori farm west of the copse of trees, was about 800 yards wide and covered by Weir's six Napoleons and nothing else. South of the Codori farm Carr's troops were slowly retiring east, turning about now and again to let loose a volley to slow down Confederate pursuit.

Turnbull was several hundred yards east of the Emmitsburg Road, retiring toward Plum Run ravine. With Carr's infantry to his front and right and Brewster's disorganized masses off to his left, he was unable to fire, for fear of hitting his own men. Ever so slowly his six guns were hauled back, loaded with double canister, each Number Four man walking backward, lanyard stretched taught. Turnbull rode up and down his line as it retired, as musketry from beyond his front knocked Humphreys's line to pieces. Then an opening—one gun was fired—then another. The double canister tore bloody holes in the Confederate line. It stopped, but only momentarily, as the Rebels closed up the gaps and continued. They pressed on, stepping over the dead and mangled bodies of their comrades and of Yankees who had not managed to get clear of Turnbull's line of fire.

To his right rear Turnbull could see Weir's gunners in action 400 yards away. The latter's guns were firing at will over Turnbull as that battery descended the Emmitsburg Road rise heading back toward the low ground northwest of Thomas. By now the Codori farmyard had been overrun as Brig. Gen. Ambrose R. Wright's Georgians scattered what remained of the Union forces defending it.[5]

Chapter 12 | "Until Hell Freezes Over"

Just before Turnbull reached Plum Run, a long line of blue appeared off Weir's left flank, advancing at quick time toward Plum Run. It was General Hancock and Captain Miller, bringing Weir's promised support. Hancock had ridden northeast, angling toward the copse of trees. He found Colonel Heath's 19th Maine at ease where they had been placed. Hancock rode up to Heath and, without explanation, ordered the colonel to follow him. At that moment there was not another infantry regiment between the 19th Maine's left flank and Colvill's right, or according to Sgt. Silas Adams, Company F, 19th Maine, "There were no troops then between its left company [F] and the First Minnesota, about sixty rods [330 yards] away." Hancock was widening one gap to fill another, gambling that his reinforcements would make it in time. With the 19th gone there would be no one between the copse of trees and the 1st Minnesota. The Hummelbaugh farm lane lay open for the taking, as did the Army Headquarters and the Taneytown Road beyond.[1]

The 19th crossed over the low stone wall, dressed ranks, and stepped off at right shoulder shift. Hancock and Heath rode together as the regiment descended the ridge angling toward Plum Run. Hancock may have spotted Turnbull's battery retiring, south of Weir, as the 19th's line of march was taking it more toward that battery than toward Weir. Hancock may even have thought they were Weir's guns. As the 19th neared Plum Run, Hancock and Heath had drifted apart, Hancock nearer the left-center, Colonel Heath the right-center. Passing within 200 yards of Weir's left-most gun, the 19th Maine continued toward the thickets along Plum Run and Turnbull beyond. Turnbull later wrote:

> We were so pressed and crowded by our own infantry I had no time to look for a way out. My concern was to save my guns from being carried off. It was after Lieutenant James sped past me when I realized we could go no further. By then it was too late as the enemy was less than one rod off my left.[2]

There was firing all around Turnbull now, and his panicky horses were snorting and rearing in their traces. Fleeing members of Sickles's Third Corps streamed past. To make matters worse, Capt. Aaron Seeley's 4th United States Light, Battery K, now under the command of Lt. Robert James after Seeley had been wounded, came careening past Turnbull's battery from the direction of the Klingle farm, making for Plum Run. Battery K had been nearly overrun at the Klingle orchard while supporting Brewster's brigade and had been ordered out by General Humphreys. James's cannoneers beat a hasty retreat north, as fast as their horses could pull the carriages. All hell broke loose as Battery K passed to the rear of Turnbull then swung east, angling toward Cemetery Ridge. Lieutenant James's frantic withdrawal created a near panic along that part of the line.

At this point Turnbull's limber teams could not be persuaded to go any further. Blocked by the thickets along Plum Run, amid the smoke and confusion, the lieutenant ordered the teams cut loose, leaving the limbers and guns west of the run. Four hundred yards north, Lieutenant Weir saw this and, with Confederates in possession of the Codori farm, ordered his guns limbered.

Rumbling back toward Cemetery Ridge, Lieutenant James led his fleeing column toward Plum Run and the advancing 19th Maine. By the time his lead gun hit the muddy run north of the farm lane, Heath's regiment was but a few yards east of it. Without slowing, James's lead gun crashed headlong through the 19th Maine's center. Swearing infantrymen dove for cover to escape the thundering hooves and body-crushing wheels of James's on-rushing battery. The six guns and two caissons, all loaded with wounded men, including Lieutenant Seeley, followed James through the gap.[3]

Hancock witnessed the collision from his position on the 19th Maine's left and spurred his horse toward the gap at top speed. James, finally realizing what he had done, slowed as Hancock approached. The general was furious. He shook his fist at the lieutenant and bellowed, "if I commanded this regiment I'd be God Damned if I would not bayonet you." With the Confederate advance just a few hundred yards away, Hancock had more pressing matters to deal with, and he turned his attention back to getting the 19th Maine started again.

With help from Colonel Heath, and Captain Miller, the 19th's ranks were soon closed, and the regiment resumed its advance, heading west-southwest toward the shallow ravine housing Plum Run.[4]

Weir, having started his battery eastward, saw what had taken place. Meanwhile, Lieutenant James had come to his senses enough to swing his leading section back around, positioning it near where the incident occurred as the balance of his battery ascended Cemetery Ridge near the Hummelbaugh farm lane. Weir likewise swung back around in "Reverse Trot," unlimbering about 100 yards north of James, 200 yards east of his previously exposed position. After sending all six caissons over the crest, Weir reopened, as did James, targeting the left wing of Lang's Florida brigade as it advanced eastward, seemingly unmolested. Still, there was too much smoke and confusion, and too many fleeing Third Corps troops to their front for their firing to be effective.

The 19th Maine crossed Plum Run and advanced perhaps another hundred yards when Hancock halted the line. Sgt. Silas Adams recalled:

> General Hancock rode along the line and jumped from his horse and took the first man on the left, who was George Durgin, and conducted him forward about a couple of rods and a little to the left. He said to Durgin, "Will you stay here?" Durgin, looked up into the General's face and replied, "I'll stay here, General, until hell freezes over."

Hancock smiled. He ordered the colonel to dress his regiment on that man, jumped on his horse and galloped away.[5]

Company F's left flank was about 40 yards to Turnbull's right rear. Hundreds of troops belonging to Brewster, Graham, Burling, and Carr's left wing retreated north-northeast through the Trostle and Klingle meadows. South of Thomas, Carr's left wing withdrew due east, passing over the rise east of the Klingle house and down toward Plum Run, west of Thomas's position. As Wilcox's line emerged over the crest of the rise, east of the Klingle farm and west of and above Plum Run, Thomas, surrounded by the smoke and the noise and the milling men, could not tell friend from foe. The two small regiments Gibbon had sent to Humphreys, the 19th Massachusetts and 42nd New York, did more harm than good as they masked Thomas's field of fire. Had the lieutenant opened at that time, it's likely he would have hit men in Gibbon's supporting column.

Placed in line of battle just east of and below the crest of the rise, the 19th and 42nd lay down and waited. Col. Arthur F. Devereux, commanding the 19th Massachusetts, wrote, "Left to ourselves, I suggested to Colonel Mallon [42nd New York] that the two regiments be formed behind the crest of a short knoll some distance in our front, there to lie down, wait until our retreating line, which was right upon us then, had passed, deliver a volley by the rear and front ranks, to check the pursuing enemy, then make good our retreat."[6] After most of Sickles's men had passed over them the two regiments rose and delivered a volley into Wilcox's 14th and 9th Alabama regiments. A second volley soon followed.

Although stung by Devereux's fire, Wilcox's line pressed on. The 19th and 42nd both retired as the Confederates crested the rise. With both flanks in the air their position was untenable. Devereaux wrote:

> It became necessary then to retreat immediately to avoid capture, the enemy line outflanking us on the right and left hundreds of yards to each side and very near—so indeed, that both regiments captured several prisoners.[7]

The 19th Massachusetts followed the 42nd New York back down the rise toward Plum Run, passing through the ravine south of Thomas's battery. They were retiring in good order, but men from other units were fleeing in disorganization and panic. North of Turnbull's battery, the 19th Maine stood fast, but as the intensity of Confederate fire increased, Colonel Heath ordered his regiment to lie down. As he did, a Third Corps officer ordered him to form his regiment to help stem the retreat. Knowing his men would be swept away if they did so, the colonel or-

Brig. Gen. Cadmus M. Wilcox
U.S. Army Military History
Institute, Carlisle, Pa.

dered the 19th Maine to stay down. Heath actually walked behind the Third Corps officer countermanding his order to stand. As Devereux and Mallon had done, Heath allowed most of the retreating Federals to pass over his regiment before ordering his men to their feet. When they rose, Col. David Lang's Florida Brigade was less than 40 yards away.[8]

Heath's New Englanders faced the 5th, 8th, and 2nd Florida regiments, from his left to right. The 5th outflanked his left by 100 yards as it angled toward Turnbull's battery while the 2nd pressed eastward far beyond his right, making for the opening between the 19th's exposed right and Weir's battery.

Delivered at about 35 yards, Heath's first volley staggered the 8th Florida. By the time his four hundred rifles had fired their second round the 8th was stopped cold. To his left, the 5th Florida was stopped in its tracks when Turnbull let loose a tremendous dose of canister and spherical case, probably set at one-half second, into their ranks at point blank range. As John Smith of the 19th Maine described it:

> In this position of some thirty yards from their lines we fired about eight rounds each into their ranks. The Battery which joined us on our left [Turnbull] commenced firing the moment the front was clear of the Third Corps. The gunners, with coats off and sleeves rolled up, were working their guns throwing shell and canister into, and making terrible havoc in the enemy ranks.[9]

Chapter 13 | The Fight for Turnbull's Battery

Having fired most of his canister during his withdrawal at fixed prolonge, and having sent away his caissons, Lieutenant Turnbull was forced to improvise a defensive measure to buy time. He ordered the fuses of his fixed spherical case and shell removed so that they would explode immediately following detonation of the powder charge. Using this technique, referred to as "Rotten Shot," the hollow iron balls would explode into jagged and lethal projectiles at the muzzle. If the round did not explode, as many did not, that ball would act as solid shot. At less then 50 yards accuracy was not a problem. This practice was rare, being nearly as hazardous to the men working the guns as to the enemy.

Turnbull was now on foot, revolver drawn, firing, urging his men on, firing again. The 5th Florida wavered as another blast from his six Napoleons tore terrible gaps in its ranks. Again his guns fired, the enemy but 30 yards off. Capt. Isaac W. Starbird, commanding Company F, 19th Maine, watched a group of Rebels dash toward the small gap between his left and Turnbull's right gun. Smith wrote, "This movement to the rear, on the left of our line, exposed the battery on our left to capture, so the guns were drawn back to conform to our movement."[1] Reacting quickly, Starbird refused his company, pulling it back to face south, matching Turnbull's movement. Although this widened the gap between the two units, Starbird could bring more weapons to bear and his concentrated musketry drove back the attackers.

Starbird's alertness and quick action bought more than just time for Turnbull. Not only did it allow the lieutenant a few minutes to drag four of his six guns back to align with Company F to his right, but at that moment one of his caisson limbers arrived with a load of ammunition. While the fixed ammunition was being dumped on the ground the center and left sections were untied from their respective limber carriages and four of the six horses from the newly arrived limber were unhitched and brought forward. They were unhitched because the thickets were too dense for limbers to get through. Two teams of two horses each were hitched to 2nd Lt. Manning Livingston's two limber carriages while the guns themselves were being attached to the pintal hooks. Within moments of re-hitching, Livingston's right section was off. Passing around the left flank of Captain Starbird's line, Lieutenant Livingston rumbled north.[2]

Livingston's guns passed behind Heath's extended line, then out into the open beyond his exposed right flank. Musketry from the 8th and 2nd Florida regiments could not stop the movement of the lieutenant's column back across Plum Run toward the spot where Hancock had initially placed Lieutenant Weir, about 300 yards east of the Codori barn. In the smoke and chaos, Livingston could see but a few yards in either direction as he passed to the west of Weir's third and present position. Here he brought his guns to a halt. Without regard for his personal safety, the lieutenant ordered his brace of smoothbores back into action about 100 yards off Weir's right flank. His intent was to continue supporting Turnbull from this position, and he reopened on the 2nd and 8th Florida at near perfect left-enfilade. This fire, added to that of Weir's six guns and Lieutenant James's two, was all that kept the 2nd Florida from enveloping the 19th Maine's right flank.[3]

The concentrated intensity of this fire forced Maj. W. R. Moore, commanding the 2nd Florida, to change his front, sending his left wing directly toward Livingston and Weir, and thus taking some pressure off the 19th Maine. While the 2nd Florida's left inched its way toward Livingston's front, a volley from the lieutenant's right rear, fired by Col. Joseph Wasden's 22nd Georgia, coming up from the direction of Codori's farmyard, slammed into the isolated section. Livingston toppled from his horse, dead. His left limber pulled away, leaving the right limber and both guns to be overrun. The two captured guns were of no immediate use to the Confederates as both of the number-one cannoneers vanished eastward with their rammers. Soldiers from the 2nd Florida and 22nd Georgia each claimed a prize and detailed men to haul their trophies back toward the Emmitsburg Road.[4]

The departure of Livingston's guns not only shortened Turnbull's line and diluted his concentrated firepower, but it also enlarged the gap between his battery and the refused left flank of Captain Starbird's company. As the 5th Florida renewed its advance toward that gap, the 2nd Florida was now able to take advantage of Colonel Heath's exposed right flank. Despite the threat, Heath held his position while Turnbull renewed his efforts to save the battery. Unnoticed by Turnbull, however, was a new threat coming off his left flank. After the 19th Massachusetts and 42nd New York withdrew, there was no organized support south of his battery. The 9th Alabama was perilously close and angling toward his left gun from the direction of the small knoll.

About a hundred yards east–southeast of Turnbull, across Plum Run, Thomas's Battery C was waiting. Because of the high thickets mentioned earlier, the lieutenant's men held their fire, unable to see beyond their masked front. Fleeing Union soldiers in front of Thomas crossed Plum Run, heading directly toward his guns. As the Federals streamed up the ridge toward him, the only thing that kept this tide from washing through the battery were the mounted section commanders and chief of pieces, who stood in front of the guns, forcing the retreating soldiers to either side. Once across Plum Run, most of these men headed east-southeast, passing to the left of Battery C, and away from the rough ground. This put them on a direct path toward Colvill's 1st Minnesota. The knoll in front of Willard's "Harpers Ferry Cowards" was crawling with fleeing blue-clad troops. To the west and drawing closer were Barksdale's Mississippians, screened by the Plum Run thickets, the undulating ground, the masses of fleeing Union troops, and the thick smoke shrouding the field. They moved unseen into the low ground west of the run and north of Trostle's barn.

After having placed Private Durgin and the 19th Maine, Hancock, accompanied by Captain Miller, re-crossed Plum Run, racing toward Thomas's battery. He rode up to the lieutenant, stopping momentarily to engage him in conversation. Both men could see Confederates en masse on the rise west of the run, heading their way. The general cautioned Thomas to watch for friendly reinforcements moving across his front as he was expecting them. In the desperate circumstance there is little doubt but that he told Lieutenant Thomas to hold at all costs. The general then spurred his horse up the meadow angling toward the crest.[5]

Hancock evidently remembered the 1st Minnesota waiting to Thomas's left rear, because he headed in that direction.

Brig. Gen. William Barksdale
U.S.A.M.H.I.

His primary goal at this point was to stop the rout of Sickles's men. Riding up to Colonel Colvill, he asked for assistance. Colvill and his officers had already tried to stop the fleeing Federals, and now they tried again, but it was no use. Colvill recalled, "By General Hancock's order, and with his personal assistance, I undertook to stop and put them [fugitives] in line; but found it impossible, and demoralizing to my own regiment in doing so."[6] Alfred Carpenter of the 1st Minnesota also remembered that "[t]he stragglers came rushing through the lines, whom we in vain tried to stop and at last gave it up entirely, believing they were more injury than help to us. Now and then shells fell uncomfortably close to us."[7]

The general spent little time with Colvill after spotting General Humphreys a short distance to the south. He and Miller rode against a rising tide of blue ascending from the thickets to their right, below where they had seen the enemy lines west of the run. He found Humphreys and his aides successfully rallying fleeing troops. A short conversation ensued in which Humphreys learned Hancock was now in command of the Third Corps. The two generals readily agreed that they needed to stop the threat at this point. Leaving Humphreys, Hancock rode on, watching Colonel De Trobriand rally troops by waving one of his regiment's battleflags.

No one had yet told General Birney that Hancock was in command of the Third Corps. As a result, Birney was riding about the ridge issuing directives as if he were in charge, certainly what he should have been doing at that time. At some point, he and Hancock probably passed when the latter rode south. Because of the smoke and confusion, and issues at hand, they apparently did not see each other. Birney ended up near the low rough ground surrounded by adjutants and aides. Here he found Colonel Brewster and General Carr, to whom he related the events that placed him in command of the Third Corps. It did not matter whether they had heard of

Hancock's temporary position or not, they would work with Birney to get the job done. The general ordered his two officers to reform their lines as fast as possible near where he was. As late as August 1st, 1863, when Carr wrote his official report, he was still under the impression that General Birney was in command of the Third Corps at that stage of the fighting. Birney rode about the field trying with little success to corral fugitives while Hancock continued south. At this time, there were no fewer then one dozen riders from Hancock's headquarters, including Bingham and Morgan, searching for officers still controlling their men in order to gather Hancock's reinforcements. [8]

To Birney's left, Humphreys and De Trobriand were still at it, and having better luck. Most of Humphreys's success was due not to his commanding figure, but rather to the 19th Massachusetts and 42nd New York. Having re-crossed Plum Run, they reformed west of the Patterson Woods on the crest of the ridge, just to the rear of where the general was trying to form his line. The two regiments acted much like provost guards, physically stopping some of the fleeing Federals, while others saw them and fell in rather then pass through. In all the excitement and chaos Hancock missed these two regiments standing idle to the rear of Humphreys's rag-tag line. Although the two regiments neither engaged nor moved forward at that time, their steadiness heartened the fugitives, many of whom joined their ranks. "In a short time we met the second line of our men pressing forward [reforming]. Passing through them a distance of perhaps 25 yards, we halted, as did the line we had just met," wrote Colonel Devereaux. "At this point the two regiments rested on a slope [Cemetery Ridge south of the 1st Minnesota] fronting the enemy, exposed to their artillery fire [probably Alexander in the Peach Orchard], which was very hot, unable to use our own fire on the columns of the enemy because of the line in front."[9]

Knowing the Emmitsburg Road line would not hold, Humphreys had stayed on until Turnbull's six Napoleons had been successfully withdrawn, or so he thought. He then rode east, rallying his line as best he could. Carr's right wing fought grudgingly, facing back numerous times not 40 yards from the advancing enemy. While many units fled north as a disorganized rabble, most of Carr's retreat on the right was organized and systematic. The organization, however, dissolved when that wing crossed over Plum Run. Many of Carr's men paid little attention to Humphreys, or anyone else for that matter, continuing instead up and over Cemetery Ridge using Hummelbaugh's Farm Lane. Those who chose to stay faced back at the base of the ridge behind the rough ground, to the right and rear of the 19th Maine.

Most of the officers from Sickles's Third Corps had performed with honor and courage. Most were now busy rallying whatever troops they could. Some cobbled together a company of men, leading them toward Humphreys, while others led as few as one or two soldiers. Still others faced back alone, some with musket in hand. Hancock could not have asked for better help than they provided, especially from the disciplined General Humphreys. "I directed General Humphreys to form his command [the line Colonel Devereux mentioned] on the ground from which General Caldwell had moved to the support of the Third Corps, which was promptly done," Hancock later recalled. "The number of his troops collected was, however, very small, scarcely equal to an ordinary battalion, but with many colors, this command being composed of the fragments of many shattered regiments."[10]

Leaving Humphreys, General Hancock continued south toward the George Weikert farm. He had not ventured far, perhaps 200 yards, when he spotted Willard's brigade, at right shoulder shift with bayonets fixed, advancing in a splendid line. Willard was leading the 125th New York, commanded by Lt. Col. Levin Crandell, and the 126th, commanded by Col. Elikim Sherrill. After having detached the 39th New York, commanded by Maj. Hugo Hildebrandt, and leaving MacDougall's 111th New York on the crest in reserve, the 125th and 126th advanced due west toward Plum Run and the lower Trostle meadows. The 39th angled away on its own to the southwest, toward the old Trostle Lane as it descended toward Plum Run west of George Weikert's farm. Hancock would later take some of the credit for Willard's positioning:

> I established Colonel Willard's brigade at the point through which General Birney's division had retired, and fronting the approach of the enemy, who were pressing vigorously on. There were no other troops on its right or left, and the brigade soon became engaged.[11]

Lt. Col. James Bull, soon to command the brigade, later wrote:

> ...by order of the division general, the brigade moved
> from its position by the left flank about a quarter
> mile toward the left of the line, where it formed in
> line of battle, and ordered by Colonel Willard to
> charge two Rebel batteries, supported by infantry,
> posted on the hill [Emmitsburg Road Rise] in front
> of the position occupied by the brigade.[12]

The 125th and 126th had started their charge near the crest of the ridge, their line surging across what appeared to be an open and level field. In fact, it was anything but. Willard soon realized he could not see over the brow of the rise ahead as it fell away, a rise he had not noted from the ridge's crest beyond and above the military crest. Willard actually thought he was attacking batteries directly opposite him on ground a little higher than his own. He did not realize he was separated from them by a ravine and creek. He had no clue that Plum Run existed. Once he got started, however, there was no turning back, and it turned ugly in a hurry.[13] "The line advanced over declining ground, through a dense underbrush extending to the base of the hill previously mentioned, in as good order as the circumstances of the case would admit, at which place [base of hill] the alignment, without stopping, was partially rectified," continued Colonel Bull. "Contrary...to the expectations of the brigade commander, the rebels [Barksdale

& Wilcox's right flank] in considerable force were found in this underbrush."[14]

Hancock wasted no time watching Willard's column disappear into Plum Run. He rode up to the front of an unidentified regiment and without formal introductions, ordered the 111th New York forward. MacDougall recalled:

> The brigade commander [Willard] ordered me to remain at the left in reserve about 200 yards in rear, when General Hancock came riding up shortly, and ordered me with my regiment to the right [North] in great haste, to charge a rebel advance, which had broken through our [Humphreys's] lines on the right of the Third Brigade, and had advanced 20 or 30 rods beyond our lines, and was in the act of turning the right flank of our brigade.[15]

Hancock had no idea of the identity of Colonel MacDougall or his regiment. He simply pointed back in the direction from which he had come and ordered the colonel to charge toward Thomas's battery. Although he did not comment on it at the time, he noted that the 1st New York, Battery B was no longer in its previous position.

The general wheeled his horse about as the 111th started forward. He rode with MacDougall a short distance. The colonel later recalled, "When ordered to stand the men sprang to their feet and we moved by the right flank and then left at the double quick."[16] With Willard gone, there is no reason to doubt that General Hancock directed and accompanied the 111th to the right. "During the movement to the right, we were under a heavy fire of shell and canister from the batteries of the enemy," recalled Capt. Aaron Seeley, who later commanded the regiment, "commingled with the bullets of a triumphant horde of rebels who had forced their way up to the position previously held by others of our Union forces, who had been compelled to give way before their attack, with the loss of four of our cannon [Turnbull]."[17]

At some point, Hancock stopped the right-flank move and ordered MacDougall in, advancing by the left-flank. Having already fixed bayonets, the regiment surged forward on MacDougall's command while the general galloped off, continuing north, the way he had come. The timing of 111th's charge had come so close to that of the 126th that men in the 126th actually thought MacDougall had charged from the rear at the same instant. That, however, was not the case. There had to have been at least a two to three minute gap between them, enough time for Willard to become isolated and very much alone.

North of the 111th, Turnbull's cannoneers were locked in bloody hand-to-hand combat as the 14th and 9th Alabama and 5th Florida closed in on them from three sides. No battery could hold its ground against such odds while fighting over such terrain. The cannoneers wielded handspikes and rammers like clubs, but it was to no avail. They did, however, have enough time to spike one gun before the left piece was overrun from the left. As Alabamans poured into the battery from the left and front, the fighting became brutal and intimate. While attempting to spike another gun, Pvt. James Riddle, a U.S. regular from Virginia, had his skull crushed by a clubbed musket while his mess mate, Pvt. George Bently, was shot through the body.[18]

Lieutenant Turnbull was luckier. After emptying his revolver, he made good his escape with 50 others, leaving behind eight enlisted men killed and a dozen wounded. North of him, Colonel Heath pulled the 19th Maine's line back as the 2nd Florida gained his right flank. "Colonel Heath received word that the enemy had made its appearance on our right flank. He ordered the Regiment to fall back and it did so in perfect order," wrote Smith. "The distance the Regiment fell back did not exceed two or three rods, when they faced the enemy again and, in perfect alignment, began firing again."[19]

By the time Heath's regiment faced about, a small group of men from Brewster's brigade had reformed off Thomas's right flank, due east of the 19th Maine. "While the Nineteenth was engaged in loading and firing, it was observed that a small body of men had formed in our rear," continued Smith. "They were waving their flags and appeared to be cheering us on in the work we had in hand. They showed no anxiety, however, to advance with us."[20]

What neither Smith nor anyone else in the 19th Maine realized at that time was that the flag waving was not intended to inspire them, but rather to signal retiring Excelsior Brigade troops. Brewster's plan worked, as about 150 of his fleeing troops flocked to and rallied around his brigade colors at the western edge of the low rough ground.[21]

While Brewster rallied his Excelsiors, Colonel Wasden's Georgians and Major Moore's Floridians spent little time celebrating the capture of Livingston's section. Urged forward again, the Georgians quickly closed on Weir's right rear while Moore's Floridians withered under his doses of double canister. Supported by other Georgians from Wright's brigade, the 22nd closed to within 30 yards of Battery C. From an impromptu firing line, Wasden's men let loose a crippling volley that smashed into Lt. Homer Baldwin's section anchoring Weir's right. Fired upon from point blank range by a line that seemed to rise out of the ground, Weir could not respond; then came another volley. A few men from Gibbon's routed line along the pike tried to reform but were driven in. Then the Georgians bayonet charged. Within moments, the 2nd Florida also surged forward, their line ragged and irregular, but nonetheless lethal.

The first volley by the 22nd had brought down Baldwin's horse. Quickly rising, he ordered his section hitched and away. This was easier said than done, as all the men on the right gun were wounded, dead, or busy defending themselves. Pvt. Peter Sharrow fell in this melee, shot through the body several times while wielding a handspike. Pvt. John Porter's spine was shattered while he attempted to hitch the right gun.[22] Baldwin, unable to do much on foot, followed his left gun as it bolted away. Lt. Charles Whitesell was less fortunate. With all his horses shot down or bayoneted, his center section sat where it was hitched.

Like Baldwin's cannoneers, Whitesell's men wielded handspikes and rammers and, as with Baldwin's command, the Confederate attack was overwhelming. When the 2nd Florida and 22nd Georgia surged out of the smoke, both lieutenants stayed only long enough to empty their revolvers; and then it was time to get out. Whitesell hoisted Baldwin onto his horse and galloped east, leaving half of Weir's battery in the hands of the enemy.

Weir was on the left with Lt. Jacob Roemer when that section pulled away. He mistakenly assumed both Whitesell and Baldwin had gotten out too, thus he prematurely left them to fend for themselves. He had not ridden far when his horse collapsed, shot from under him. In the meantime Roemer's brace of guns thundered past, cresting the ridge somewhere north of Hummelbaugh's farm lane. Bruised from the fall, the lieutenant slowly began to rise when there was a dull thud and down he went again. Weir had been struck in the forehead by a spent round. Others stopped to lend a hand as he lay dazed. Helped to his feet, he slowly made his way toward James's section thinking it was Roemer. He turned back in time to witness vicious hand–to–hand fighting for some guns. It did not register that they belonged to him. Dazed and confused, Weir staggered up Cemetery Ridge. There, he noted the section under Lieutenant James rumbling off, heading east, entering Hummelbaugh's farm lane near the base of the ridge. He also noted another battery to his immediate left [north] as it swung around at "reverse trot." It was the missing

1st New York Battery B, returning.[23]

Having gone back into battery after crashing through the 19th Maine, Lieutenant James reopened on Lang's column. His engagement is not documented. At some point during this engagement, probably about the time Weir's battery was being dismantled, James was approached by Capt. Nathaniel Irish, temporarily assigned to General Hunt's staff, who happened by on an errand to recruit guns for Colonel McGilvery's artillery line along Trostle's Lane. James hesitated, until Colonel Warner interceded. He confirmed Irish's order, and James followed Captain Irish back to the Taneytown Road, then south toward the George Weikert farm lane.

With Weir out of the fight, and James gone, there were no organized Federal units left on this part of the field. Brewster had men regrouping, but not enough to be a credible force. To Brewster's rear, General Carr was having a time of it. Gibbon's division could no longer be counted on for support as regiment after regiment had been detached until there was nothing left. Gibbon's regiments and artillery near the copse of trees had their own hands full and were themselves sending off couriers in search of reinforcements.

All was not well with the Confederates at this point either. The 2nd Florida's left wing had sustained heavy casualties and could not immediately press its advantage. Detaching several dozen men to drag back Livingston's and Weir's five captured guns did not help. Major Moore's left had by now broken down into small groups, as had the right of Colonel Wasden's 22nd Georgia, the latter having unwound as it moved through the Codori farmyard. The Confederate line immediately north of the 19th Maine was, at this time, a mixed bag from several regiments clustered together in small bunches—too disorganized to press forward.

Brewster noted this disorganization as he readied his 150 effectives. Behind him, Maj. Charles Hamlin, General Carr's assistant adjutant-general, had assembled nearly 100 more from that division. When it eventually registered on Weir, who had returned to the base of the ridge, that James's guns were not his, and those that remained on the field were, he approached Hamlin. Pointing back toward Whitesell's and Baldwin's guns, Weir pleaded with the major to get them back. In his battered state, Weir was in no shape to help. Instead, after speaking with Hamlin, he came upon Baldwin's left piece sitting idle near the Lane. He was handed the reins to a horse and led that piece to safety, still not knowing the fate of his half–battery.[24]

South of Brewster, Turnbull had made it back to the safety of Thomas's line. His entire battery had been overrun and captured, although it is doubtful he knew what had happened to Livingston. His first order of business was to see that the enemy did not carry off his four guns west of the run. At Turnbull's request, Thomas ordered all six of his smoothbores to train on the overrun battery. Wheeling slightly half–right en echelon, all six reopened with double canister—at about 100 yards. After the first round Thomas switched to spherical case, or shrapnel, then back to canister. Within moments, one of Turnbull's Napoleons had been destroyed and the remaining three carriages so mangled they were rendered useless. The 14th and 9th Alabama regiments milled about the battery, cowering from Thomas's canister and shrapnel. Not only could they not drag off their trophies, they were powerless to return effective fire. The men of the 5th Florida's right flank also came under Thomas's fire as they tried to close on Plum Run between the battery and the rough ground. Instead, they were forced to go to ground, seeking shelter behind whatever cover they could find.[25]

The canister and shrapnel from Thomas's guns stopped the Confederates to his immediate front and right–front, but not those north of him. Portions of the 8th Florida managed to reach Plum Run after a slowly progressing battle with Heath in which they sustained terrible casualties. The 19th Maine again faced back in a line nearly parallel with Thomas's gun line. The two regiments stood but yards apart, sending volley after volley crashing across the run into each other. For just the slightest moment, Colonel Heath saw what he thought was the 8th Florida's center beginning to waver. Heath ordered concentrated fire on their colors as the bearer waved them defiantly a few yards away.[26]

Chapter 14 | Hancock Rides North

Having sent in the 111th, Hancock and Captain Miller galloped north, passing back over the dry ravine, east of and above its intersection with Plum Run. They spurred their horses into the open meadow in front of and below Humphreys's reforming line. A line of infantry was moving toward them, having just emerged from the thickets south of Thomas. They were perhaps 50 yards distant and Hancock could see they were Confederates. The Rebels saw them at the same instant, several raising their rifles and firing. "Proceeding along the line, I met a regiment of the enemy, the head of whose column was about passing through an unprotected interval in our line," recalled Hancock. "A fringe of undergrowth in front of our line offered facilities for it to approach very close to our lines without being observed. It was advancing firing, and had already twice wounded my aide, Captain Miller."[1]

The 11th Alabama had punched through General Carr's left at the Klingle farm after helping the 10th Alabama rout Seeley's 4th U.S Battery K. The 10th had carried the road to the right of the 11th, driving back whatever portions of Brewster's line that had not been carried away by Barksdale. Pressing Carr and Brewster's crumbling line before them, the two Alabama regiments advanced through the Klingle farm and into Trostle's meadows. Several determined stands and one counter-charge slowed but did not stop the 11th and, as resistance crumbled, their eastward momentum gathered steam. The 10th Alabama, however, met stiffer opposition as it began its descent toward the low ground east of the road. The 10th Alabama had not traveled far when its extreme right flank met Willard's advancing troops. While the 10th was engaging the 126th New York's far right, the 11th Alabama, after beating back the 26th Pennsylvania's counter–charge, shifted a bit to the south, moving instinctively toward the weakest point, a yawning gap between Thomas's battery and the advancing 111th New York's right flank. Unobstructed, the 11th Alabama's right center passed into the gap north of the 10th Alabama's left. Portions of the 11th reached Plum Run in hot pursuit of the fleeing Federals. From where these men entered Plum Run Ravine, they could not see the 111th New York starting their charge. Instead, they passed through the brush and thickets bordering the west bank, and stepped into the boggy ground of the run.

These were the men Hancock had spotted on the rise while chatting with Thomas. Ordering the wounded Miller to flee up and over the ridge, Hancock made good his own escape by galloping north–northeast, away from Plum Run and the dry ravine. He was heading directly for the 1st Minnesota, the last of his available reserves along that part of the line. By the time Hancock reached the crest, Humphreys's line was sending a spattering of shots toward the line below. The men from 11th Alabama who had passed through the ravine stopped to return fire, breaking their forward momentum. This hesitation would be all Hancock needed.

By now, MacDougall's 111th was descending the western slope of the knoll, having crossed the dry ravine south of where it intersects Plum Run. Thus far the charge was a going well—the unit was holding together. Not a man dropped from the ranks as they brushed past Third Corps fugitives still fleeing eastward. "The ground over which the first charge was made was sort of a swale [dry ravine], covered by rocks, thickly interspaced with bushes, scrub oak, and trees [the knoll]," wrote Captain Seeley. "Beyond was open ground, ascending to the west [the rise west of Plum Run]."[2] Having reached and passed over the crest of the rise, south of the dry ravine, MacDougall and his boys could now see the Plum Run ravine directly below, with portions of the 10th Alabama approaching from about 40 yards distant.

No command was needed. The 111th New Yorkers raised their rifles as they reached the edge of the precipitous slope, above the run, and let loose a volley into the faces of the 10th Alabama's left–center. At almost the same instant, MacDougall's far right opened an enfilading fire into the right flank of the 11th Alabama, in and east of the run. This flank fire slowed the 11th Alabama's right and forced it to change direction. The gray–clad men below the 111th's right, north of where the dry ravine intersects Plum Run, were caught in a bad place. The New Yorkers seemingly rose up out of the ground and now, ten feet above them, were pouring in devastating fire at almost point blank range. Through the smoke and confusion,

MacDougall could faintly see the 126th New York's flag above the 10th Alabama, and Barksdale's Mississippians beyond. By this time, the colonel's line had assumed a crescent shape, following the contour of the knoll above the run. The 111th let loose a second volley into the 10th Alabama's left with terrible effect. Confederates staggered and fell. This volley stopped them in their tracks.

From beyond the 10th another column appeared in the smoke. This was Col. Hillary A. Herbert's 8th Alabama, angling northward, away from the 126th New York and Willard's principal line, moving past the 10th toward the 11th Alabama's right–rear. Colonel Herbert's regiment moved unhindered past the 10th, changing direction more to the east. His right wing slipped into the gap between the 10th and 11th, instinctively swinging east to join in the fight. The balance of that regiment continued over the rise west of the run and into the gap between the 11th's left and the 14th Alabama's right. This additional manpower allowed the 11th Alabama to fend off MacDougall's far right as well as Humphreys's fugitives on the crest. Once again the Confederate surged forward, breaking out of the thickets about 200 yards from Thomas's left front.

Chapter 15 | "Advance and Take Those Colors"

From the crest of Cemetery Ridge, "Smoke shut the combatants from sight and we could only judge of the direction of the fight by the sound," wrote Alfred Carpenter.[1] Clouds of billowing, stinging smoke hung close to the ground in the breezeless air. Rising slowly above the treetops, it eventually drifted skyward in straight plumes, reaching as far as the eye could see. It was thick and dark, rich with the smell of cordite. The veterans in the 1st Minnesota had smelled that nauseating stench before—it was the smell of death. Although they could not see most of the field, it was obvious to all that they would be called upon in short order.

The unceasing roar of musketry was deafening. In many places only the flickering of a discharged weapon was visible. One individual shot was all but impossible to distinguish from another. Several rifled muskets were later picked up having five to ten rounds rammed home but never discharged. Such was the chaos that reigned across the field, and it was headed toward Colvill's 1st Minnesota.

Hancock rode hard up the ridge after having crossed over the dry ravine, away from the advancing 11th Alabama. His escape route carried him directly toward the reformed 1st Minnesota, 300 yards away. At some point between Hancock's conversation with General Humphreys, and his leading the 111th New York forward, the 1st Minnesota had advanced to the military crest. It is not known if an unidentified officer directed Colvill to do so or if the colonel did it on his own. Whatever the case, Colonel Colvill was in the process of reforming his regiment, south of Thomas, when Hancock approached. It was after 6:00 P.M. when the general spotted the colonel's towering figure. "I rode on rapidly through a depression in the ground close in front of them [Enemy] uninjured, and immediately met a regiment of infantry coming down from the 2nd Corps, by flank, no doubt sent there by General Gibbon or other commander in the 2nd Corps, to repair damage which had been made apparent in that direction," Hancock recalled, years after the war.[2]

There was no time for formalities. Hancock exploded with, "My God! Are these all the men we have here?" Perhaps he was disappointed that with all the Third Corps troops who had fled through this position, Colvill had not managed to stop any. Perhaps he had hoped that some of the reinforcements he had called on would have arrived by then. It also sounds as if he did not recognize Colvill, though this is unlikely, as he had ordered the man placed under arrest not 48 hours earlier.

One thing is certain. Hancock realized how critical was the moment, and how few men there were to seize upon it. By now the 11th Alabama's center, reinforced by the 8th, was skirmishing up the meadow, having passed through the run. The added strength allowed the Confederates to emerge from the thickets as one irregular line of several hundred men. Hancock knew he had to hold the Taneytown Road if Cemetery Hill was to be held. It was also the key to holding the Baltimore Pike. Hancock pointed to the west–southwest, back toward the enemy line that had fired on him. They were less than 300 yards away. Reportedly, his last words to Colvill were: "Advance, Colonel, and take those colors."[3]

The general stayed only long enough to hear Colvill address his regiment with "Forward double-quick." "I directed that commander of that regiment to attack the enemy troops displaying the colors very close by, with directions to take it at once," Hancock later wrote under calmer circumstances. "I had no alternative but to order the regiment in…I saw in some way five minutes must be gained or we were lost." By now, portions of the 8th and 11th Alabama regiments had gained a foothold in the meadow beyond Thomas's left and MacDougall's right. Trading long–range volleys with Humphreys's small line, they instinctively angled away toward the east-northeast, where resistance was weakest. A few yards further north, the 14th and 9th Alabama regiments had their hands full with Thomas's double canister and shrapnel. They also had Brewster's New Yorkers to contend with when his orphans moved forward into the rough ground, forming an irregular line between Thomas's right and the 19th Maine's left.[4]

Eight hundred yards to the south, Colonels McGilvery and Warner had managed to patch together a makeshift line of 30 cannons. Placing them west of the crest, just south of

Willard, they reopened and battered Confederates from south of Willard all the way to Trostle's Woods, south of the lane. Their concentrated firepower helped stabilize the crumbling Union line in that sector, with minimal infantry support. Twenty-four of them were now blasting Barksdale's left flank into submission and, with help from Willard's newly arrived 39th, 125th, and 126th New York regiments, plus rallying Third Corps infantry, they solidified the line on Cemetery Ridge south of Willard. The effect of this was simple. With Barksdale's Mississippians fagged out, and Lang's Floridians nearly so, Wilcox's brigade was caught in a natural pocket with little flank support. Hancock did not realize this, of course, as he did not know the ground. At this juncture, the terrain itself was responsible for slowing the Confederates as much as Union muskets.[5]

Having reformed, the veterans of the 1st Minnesota broke into double-quick on Colvill's command, advancing with arms at right shoulder shift, surging toward the approaching Rebel line. They had not traveled 20 of the 300 yards when balls began to "whiz" and "zing" past their ears. The enemy's first volley, fired from below, mostly passed overhead. Within a few steps, however, the first sickening "thuds" of impact were heard as men were knocked off their feet. The farther down the ridge the 1st Minnesota descended, the more costly it became. By the time they had traveled 100 of the 300 yards separating them from the enemy, Colvill's already thin ranks were being decimated. "It seemed as if every step was over some fallen comrade. Yet no man wavers, every gap is closed up...bringing down their bayonets, the boys press forward in unbroken line," recalled one survivor. "Men stumbled and fell. Some stayed down but others got up and continued."[6] Another Minnesotan recalled, "Bullets whistled past us; shells screeched over us; canister [shrapnel] fell among us; comrade after comrade dropped from the ranks; but on the line went. No one took a second look at the fallen companion. We had no time to weep."[7]

When Wilcox's advanced line stopped to discharge their weapons, their forward momentum was gone. From the 10th Alabama on the right, below and engaged with the 111th New York, to the 9th Alabama 300 yards north, battling Brewster's brigade and Thomas's battery, Wilcox's regiments began to pile up in the low ground along Plum Run below the rise, forming in an isolated pocket with no one off either flank. Only the 11th Alabama, and portions of the 8th, were still advancing, piling up in the lightly defended gap between Thomas and the 111th New York.[8]

Into this gap charged the 1st Minnesota on a collision course with the 11th Alabama, the center of Wilcox's line. Moving west-southwest, Colvill's men descended the ridge to the left of Thomas's battery, at slight right angles to Plum Run, their left flank angling toward the intersecting dry ravine below MacDougall. Colvill knew he had no choice but press on. They would either close on the emerging enemy and make contact or die in the open plain above them. Colvill could make out the form of another line emerging from the run. Portions of the 8th Alabama, having descended the rise west of the run, now stood above it, their upper bodies visible beyond the thickets. They let loose a volley that tore up the earth around the Minnesotans feet. Colvill wrote: "Their second line coming up immediately after, delivered a heavy fire through the remnants of their first line killing more of their own men than ours, and then we charged."[9]

The shock of an unexpected volley delivered from behind created confusion in the already chaotic ranks of the 11th Alabama, giving Colvill the moment he needed. Now was the time, impact was imminent. Almost as one, the veterans of the 1st Minnesota brought down their arms, and when within 30 yards of the enemy, delivered a crippling fire into their faces which broke the first (11th Alabama) line. Then the colonel shouted above the din..."Charge!" With bayonets leveled, the 1st Minnesota surged toward the eastern bank of Plum Run and the disorganized Confederates. The survivors of the 11th Alabama tumbled back into Plum Run, creating chaos and panic. Men turned and ran, struggling up the far bank, stopping those of the 8th Alabama who were then moving into the creek bottom to join them. Another volley by the 8th Alabama hit the 11th as the lines crashed together. Colvill took advantage of Wilcox's confusion. Having gained Plum Run his small command delivered volley after deadly volley into the disorganized gray–clad ranks.

From the thicket above the eastern bank of the creek, the 1st Minnesota delivered several volleys, its men firing at will. The North Woodsmen's fire was now hitting men of the 8th Alabama, partially exposed above the west bank. It was all but impossible for them to return accurate fire tangled up with their brethren below. Continuing forward, ever so slowly, the colonel led his men into the run, crashing through the brush and thickets, bayoneting and clubbing their way forward. Colonel Colvill urged his men on as the Confederates in the run pushed and clawed their way through the thickets on the west bank, facing back to pitch in with the 8th.

Colvill and company soon found themselves in possession of the Plum Run ravine. There would be no cheering or a hearty–hoorah. The job was far from complete. The creek bottom offered little cover for Colvill's men, and now those who had been caught in it moments before faced back with a vengeance. Confederate officers could be heard rallying the broken line as it emerged from the thickets. Soon the reinforced Alabamians west of Plum Run settled down to some disciplined shooting as that line began to make use of its elevated position. Not to be outdone, however, the 1st Minnesota held steady, firing independently as cool and calm as if on the parade ground. "I never saw cooler work done on either side, and the destruction was awful," recalled Colvill with a shudder.[10]

From kneeling and prone positions, Colvill's men laid down a deliberate fire using the west bank of the Run and its thickets for cover. The smoke lay thick and dense in the run, and with no breeze to speak of, visibility was dreadful. Men fired at muzzle flashes, or at the legs or feet of the enemy, "which was about all we could see of them at the time, as all above their knees was covered with the smoke from their own guns," recalled James Wright of the 1st Minnesota.[11] The work was hot and close and bloody, and they took as many casualties as they dished out. It was a shooting match of epic proportion, and it was fast becoming a simple case of numbers.

Although portions of both the 8th and 11th Alabama were off either flank of the 1st Minnesota, at no time did they get behind them or enfilade them. The natural curve of Plum Run as it swung southwest toward Trostle's meadows below the knoll and the battling 111th New York, was part of the reason. Colvill's line formed an inverted crescent with the enemy off both flanks either west of or in the run.[12]

The 1st Minnesota's momentum had carried them 200 yards past Thomas's left flank. The gap between Thomas's left gun, and Colvill's right, was covered by enough of Humphreys's fugitives to lay down a flank-covering fire. None of those fugitives, however, were willing to advance beyond Thomas's gun line.[13] Their added musketry was not directed at the line then engaging Colvill anyway, but rather at the men of the 14th Alabama as they floundered in and about Turnbull's disabled battery north and west of Colvill. The left flank of the 8th Alabama had actually continued toward the 14th's shattered right flank, north of the 11th, perhaps thinking Turnbull's guns an easy prize. They found out quickly that they had entered a death trap. Canister from Thomas's six cannons ripped huge holes in their lines as it had the 14th and 9th Alabama, tearing their unit apart.

Lieutenant Turnbull, now a spectator, watched as round after round was poured into the thickets. "Watching Lt. Thomas's duel reminded me of Ransom's [Fifth U.S. Battery

C] fight at Antietam—the enemy no more than 100 yards off. Although they did not advance beyond the thicket, their fire wounded a dozen men," he recalled. "[The]…section changed front in order to support the line on the left, then back, driving the enemy out of the ravine and away from my disabled battery. I later walked to where I lost my guns and was sickened by the destruction in the ravine."[14] The guns belonging to Thomas's left section wheeled slightly left–oblique in order to front and cover what remained of the gap between them and the 1st Minnesota. This move, along with the musketry from Humphreys's irregular line, stopped the left elements of the 8th and 11th Alabama regiments from penetrating beyond Colvill's right flank, and wrapping around the isolated dwindling pocket in Plum Run.

Chapter 16 | The Line Is Saved

General Wilcox described his brigade's approach to Plum Run: "On the far side of the pike the ground was descending for some 600 or 700 yards. At the bottom of this descent was a narrow valley, through which ran a rocky ravine or stream, fringed with small trees and undergrowth and bushes. Beyond this, the ground rose rapidly for some 200 yards, and upon this ridge were numerous batteries of the enemy."[1]

There is little doubt that Wilcox spotted guns on Cemetery Ridge after crossing the road. as those that had retired from the Peach Orchard were massing near the Weikert farm. It is unlikely, however, that more than a section engaged his line from Cemetery Ridge from east of the Emmitsburg Road. It is probable that what Wilcox saw and was speaking of were the combined 12 guns of Seeley and Turnbull massed on the Emmitsburg Road. These guns had targeted his Alabamians as they advanced from Seminary Ridge. To add to this fire, Weir's six guns had initially fronted that way as well.

Wilcox continued: "The ridge to my right rose into a succession of higher ridges or spurs of mountains increasing in height to the right." Highest of these mountains was Big Round Top, then Little Round Top north of it, but the one that caused him the greatest concern was the knoll from which the 111th New York was pouring its fire into the 10th Alabama. Wilcox did not state how these ridges played a role in his advance and withdrawal. The rise, or ridge, that first caused Wilcox great discomfort was the Peach Orchard area and Emmitsburg Road rise, until he secured the latter. Once on that ridge, the knoll east of the Klingle farm came into play. It blocked his view of everything north of that farm as his regiments dropped into Trostle's meadow east of the road. Cemetery Ridge to his front was but one more of the succession of ridges he had to deal with.

From Wilcox's position in the rear of his brigade, east of the Emmitsburg Road, the view of Cemetery Ridge was very deceptive. As one drops off the Emmitsburg Road, which is physically higher than Cemetery Ridge, the knoll east of the Klingle farm creates the illusion that the ground ahead is higher than the ground behind. This illusion carries east, across Plum Run. In fact, Cemetery Ridge is two feet lower than the Emmitsburg Road rise.[2]

Whatever the reason that Wilcox mentioned the heights and the succession of ridges, he was right about one thing. Once his Alabamians descended into the low ground east of the Emmitsburg Road, the rest of their fight was uphill. Col. William H. Forney's 10th Alabama had their hands full as they exchanged fire with MacDougall's New Yorkers looming above them on the knoll. They had started the day with 282 rifles. Although their ranks had been thinned already in the attack they were, nevertheless, making MacDougall's men pay dearly for their Harpers Ferry redemption. MacDougall had started with 390 rifles and had lost only a few men during the initial charge, but by this point the 111th New York had suffered 150 casualties. A steady stream of MacDougall's wounded staggered and limped back toward the crest, to the relative sanctuary of Patterson's Woods.

Many of the wounded in MacDougall's ranks refused to leave as long as they could still fire their weapons. Most of his dead, and many of his wounded, had been shot through the upper body or head, the result of the southerners firing at them from below, with the accompanying tendency to fire high. Atop MacDougall's knoll, the disciplined New Yorkers fired volley after volley into the narrow rocky valley. The close-range battle of attrition was enshrouded in acrid smoke that clung low to the ground and trees, making it hard to see anything but muzzle flashes.

MacDougall's superior firepower and position were beginning to take effect as Forney's line wavered. The veteran 10th Alabama was caught in a desperate situation. Its left wing was shot to pieces, and the surviving Rebels began falling back across the ravine, carrying with them most of Forney's center and a good portion of his right. This general withdrawal also carried back much of the 8th and 11th Alabama. Forney had already been hit twice, though both wounds were slight. As he was rallying his men near Plum Run, south of the dry ravine, he was struck a third time, a minié ball shattering his right arm. With their commander out of the fight, and all other officers down, the regiment's chain of command broke down. The unit withered away as men retired from the ranks or fell from the unrelenting fire from Thomas's Napoleons, the 1st Minnesota, and the 111th New York.[3]

Off MacDougall's left–front, the 126th New York was battling Barksdale's Mississippians and what remained of the 10th Alabama's far right flank where it had penetrated between the 126th and 111th. That small gap had opened because the 126th was forty to fifty yards in advance of and below the 111th. The men of the 10th Alabama saw this weak point and penetrated into it. Their advance was short-lived. What had looked like an opportunity proved to be a death trap. The men of MacDougall's left flank lowered their rifles and, with fixed bayonets, charged down the gentle slope into the 10th Alabama's far right flank. Confederates tumbled back upon themselves in near panic as the line gave way, men scattering in broken bunches.

Back through Trostle's meadows they tumbled, joining other fugitives from their center and left, as well as from the 8th and 11th. As they fell back the 126th New York rolled forward like a wave, breaking from right to left [north to south], washing away what remained of the 10th Alabama's right. One of the first Confederates captured during this counter–charge was the seriously wounded Colonel Forney.[4]

South of the 111th, Colonel Willard's bayonet charge drove Barksdale's survivors back across Plum Run and into the lower meadows. Like Colonel Forney, General Barksdale was also wounded, shot from his horse near Plum Run and, like Colonel Forney, was captured. Forney was fortunate. He survived; but Barksdale did not. The feisty general died the following morning in a Union hospital.

By this time Colonel McGilvery's first line of five cannons was blazing away at Barksdale's right as it obliqued past, heading north–northeast, offering an almost perfect right-enfilade to the blue–clad gunners. The Mississippian's right flank was shot to pieces as it descended into Plum Run just moments before the 125th New York slammed into it. As Barksdale spurred his horse, urging on his men, his line wrapped around toward the run, following the contour of the low rocky flood plain, striking Plum Run and the 126th New York head on.

Several hundred yards south, along the old Trostle Lane, the 39th New York battled Barksdale's orphaned 21st Mississippi Regiment, commanded by Col. Benjamin G. Humphreys. Sent in that direction on a plea from Colonel Warner, Hildebrandt's Garibaldi Guards encountered Lt. Samuel Peeples, section commander, 5th United States Artillery, Battery I (Watson). Peeples stood alone, eyes fixed on the Mississippians who moments earlier had overrun his battery.

Humphreys's Mississippians held an isolated position with the battery south of the old Trostle Lane [not north as Watson's monument indicates today—the new avenue was shifted, not the placement of the monument]. Hildebrandt's counter–charge did not come as a surprise to Humphreys, but there was little he could do. His men were simply too tired to continue forward, or hold back the charge, much less drag back their captured prizes. In addition, the regiments to his right, belonging to General Wofford, were beginning to withdraw, which would have left his regiment completely separated and further isolated.

The 39th stopped 100 yards short of the 21st Mississippi and joined in with Lt. Edwin Dow's four 12-Pound Napoleons and Lt. Albert Sheldon's four 10-Pounder Parrots from the 1st New York, Battery B, who were then pounding Humphreys's line with canister and shell at nearly point–blank range. After a few volleys, the batteries ceased firing, and the 39th charged. Nearly a year had elapsed since their ignominious surrender. Redemption was at hand. It was here, along the old Trostle lane, that "Remember Harpers Ferry" was first heard.

The 39th carried the road and battery, regaining Peeple's four cannon, then pressed on, slowly but methodically forcing back the 21st Mississippi. After the battle, Colonel Humphreys suggested that his men were not driven back, but withdrew because of Wofford's departure and were thus following his order to retire. Their disengagement, however it came about, freed Dow's battery to face about and join in against Barksdale as that line withdrew as well. Almost certainly, some of Dow's shells struck among Wilcox's retreating troops 500 yards distant.

Now it was MacDougall's turn. With the Confederate line below him in chaos and near panic, he seized the moment, and charged. Down off the knoll he led them, sword raised, the left-center following him first, the right wing following suit. Without orders, the far left wheeled to the right in order to maintain its connection with the center, capturing dozens of prisoners in the process. The far right of the line was the last to go, moving down the knoll and over the dry ravine to the immediate front and left of the 1st Minnesota.

Brig. Gen. Andrew A.
Humphreys
National Archives

MacDougall's line was now moving north-northwest, toward the knoll west of the run and Turnbull's lost battery, scooping up prisoners by the scores.

The portion of Wilcox's line still battling between MacDougall's far right flank and Thomas's left was now concentrating its fire on the remnants of the 1st Minnesota in the ravine. Colvill's men had thus far held their ground, fighting desperately from behind whatever cover could be had. Over 100 enlisted men lay dead or wounded in the smoke-filled Plum Run, and it was not over. Colonel Colvill himself was down with a jagged hole through his left shoulder and a shattered right foot. Lt. Col. John Adams lay near him, unconscious from loss of blood. Hit six times, he would survive. Maj. Mark Downie and Capt. Joseph Periam, Company K, were also down. Capt. Louis Muller, Company E, was dead, as was Lt. Waldo Farrar of Company I. Lieutenants Thomas Sinclear, Company B, James DeGray, Company G, David Demarest, Company E, and George Boyde, Company I, had also suffered severe wounds, leaving only two field officers unhurt.[6]

Some of the fire hitting the 1st Minnesota's left came, not from Wilcox, but from behind Colvill's flank, from the meadow beyond the dry ravine. This was friendly fire. The impromptu line Humphreys had cobbled together was now approaching Plum Run, firing as it advanced. Union General Andrew A. Humphreys cheered his men as they closed on the Run immediately south of Colvill, firing toward the partially obscured figures in the smoke. Caught up in General Humphreys's excitement, Capt. William H. Fernal, 12th New Hampshire Volunteers, yelled, "Come on boys," while brandishing his sword over his head. Followed by several dozen men, he charged down the slope toward the run, angling toward Colvill's left flank.

In the ravine, Capt. Nathan S. Messick of Company G, 1st Minnesota, had assumed command of the 50 or so survivors. These few could neither advance nor retreat. All they could do was return fire from within the cover of their enclave. The murderous fire from west of the run began to subside as the charge of the 111th New York struck what remained of the 10th Alabama's left, rolling it up and caving in the right flanks of the 11th and 8th, which in turn began crowding their own centers as men recoiled from the New Yorkers's furious assault. Some of Colvill's men took advantage of this confusion to make good their escape from the ravine, a few dragging or carrying wounded back with them. Lt. Christian Heffelfinger, one of the surviving officers, stood up and was immediately shot through the body. Although enemy firing was slackening, it had not ceased. Cheering, many of Colvill's men stood up to fire, reload as fast as they could, and fire again as Mac-Dougall's 111th New York drove into the retiring Alabamans to their immediate front, followed by General Humphreys passing through the regiment on the left.

The contour of the ground and the course of the run west of and below the knoll guided the 111th New York's charge across the front of the decimated 1st Minnesota. MacDougall's "Harpers Ferry Cowards" were joined by men from Birney's and Humphreys's divisions who had seized the opportunity and moved forward, passing across the dry ravine into Plum Run and through what was left of the 1st Minnesota. The 10th Alabama's rout was complete when Colonel Forney's survivors withdrew up the rise and over the crest, taking all of the 8th and the rest of 11th Alabama regiments with them. MacDougall's line did not stop in front of the 1st Minnesota but charged past, scooping up more prisoners as they went. All told, about 225 men from the 111th crossed Plum Run, charging toward the Codori farm in the far distance. MacDougall's regiment left at least 100 dead and wounded on that knoll.[5]

The 14th Alabama was the next to give way as MacDougall's line approached Turnbull's battery. General Humphreys's small line had by now entered the 1st Minnesota's position in the Run, slowing as it picked its way through the carnage. Once across, his irregular line pushed through the thickets toward the base of the rise, angling toward Turnbull's guns. Thomas bellowed "Cease Fire" in that direction when the right of Humphreys's line, lagging to the rear of the center, charged across the open meadow to his left front. Thomas quickly realigned his left section and reopened due west, targeting what remained of the 14th and 9th Alabama regiments, hurling shot and case toward the crest of the rise west of Turnbull's vacated battery.

MacDougall's and Humphreys's lines brushed past Turnbull's abandoned guns where dozens of mangled bodies lay twisted in death. What was left of the 14th Alabama and portions of the 9th melted back over the rise with the 8th, 10th, and 11th, retiring toward the Klingle farmyard 300 yards distant. The left of the 9th and portions of the 5th Florida's right, however, had retired from the battery only a short distance before facing back to confront Brewster's line. Both these wings had been shattered by Thomas's canister as they tried in vain to control the brass guns belonging to Turnbull. They left behind three of the bloodied prizes while dragging off a fourth. After hauling it a short distance, with the 111th New York closing in, they abandoned the cannon, turned, and fled.

Although a small portion of the left wing of the 9th Alabama and all of the 5th Florida had crossed Plum Run north of Turnbull, they could not exploit their advanced position. Their detached right flank was in the air, and was being pounded by all six of Thomas's Napoleons. To the north, Brewster's fire raked the rough ground east of the Run. Had King's Alabamans and Gardner's Floridians managed to break through, they would have had an open avenue to the Hummelbaugh farm lane and the rear of Thomas's battery. As it was, Brewster's 150 men blocked their way. This small line not only helped stop King's 9th Alabama, but also helped stop portions of the 5th Florida, and this in turn took some heat off the 19th Maine's left flank.

Heath's New Englanders were as busy as Brewster's New Yorkers with their own fight. Noting a slackening of musketry to their front, both Heath and Brewster correctly surmised that the enemy was about to pull back. Both increased their fire as the 5th and 8th Florida prepared to make good their withdrawal.

When Heath ordered his regiment forward, Brewster's line followed. Carr, who was down to a hundred men, started forward following Brewster. This was no hell-bent-for-leather charge. Heath's men advanced slowly, firing deliberately, loading, advancing, and firing in a steady sequence of well-aimed volleys. On one occasion Colonel Heath ordered a portion of his line to concentrate its fire on the 8th Florida color bearer who, during his advance goaded the New Englanders by tossing the flag staff ahead of him, sticking it in the ground, advancing, plucking it up, and then repeating the process. The 8th Florida's colors dropped.[7]

With the collapse of Wilcox's line, Colonel Lang's Floridians were in a hopeless position. Heath and Brewster held a superior position west of the low rough ground. Although Heath's men stood in the open on the edge of the hollow they were lower than any of Lang's regiments so that many of the Confederate rounds passed overhead. Brewster, for his part, had the advantage of slight cover from inside the low rough ground. There was more bad news for Lang, as he reported:

> While engaged in reforming here [Plum Run], an
> aide from the right informed me that a heavy force

had advanced upon General Wilcox's brigade, and was forcing it back. As the same time a heavy fire of musketry was poured upon my brigade from the woods [Rough Ground] 50 yards immediately in front, which was gallantly met and handsomely replied to by my men.[8]

As handsome as their fire may have been, it was not nearly as effective as Lang thought. His men were firing downhill and most of their rounds plowed into the earth short of their target or flew harmlessly overhead. Lang continued:

A few moments later, another messenger from my right informed me that General Wilcox had fallen back, and the enemy was then some distance in rear of my right flank. Going to my right, I discovered that the enemy had passed me more than 100 yards, and were attempting to surround me. I immediately ordered my men back to the road, some 300 yards to the rear.[9]

These were MacDougall's and Humphreys's combined lines passing beyond Turnbull's guns.

From within the low rough ground Brewster's right overlapped Heath's left, forcing his regiment to angle west-southwest toward Turnbull's battery. This dropped Brewster farther behind the 19th Maine. Carr's line angled away from Brewster as he advanced to the west-northwest, seeking to clear Heath's right flank. Carr's line also fell behind as it angled away. Ahead of them, the 8th Florida received orders to pull back and began a slow and deliberate withdrawal, leaving their fallen color-bearer and his flag lying in the dirt. They turned around as individuals and in small groups to discharge their weapons—the 19th Maine cautiously following but pressing no harder than the 8th Florida resisted. The 5th Florida, and what remained of the 9th Alabama's left flank, pulled back, some of the men passing Turnbull's battery as Thomas ceased fire for fear of hitting his own men as they too closed on the abandoned guns.

Closing on the thickets, where the dead color–bearer lay, the 19th Maine passed over the 8th Florida's flag. No one in either of Heath's two battle lines bothered to pick it up. Little thought was given to the downed prize until several of the men, after having crossed Plum Run, glanced back. According to Colonel Heath, one of Brewster's New Yorkers picked it up and was carrying it off triumphantly, waving it as he disappeared back toward the ridge. That was not Brewster's recollection of the event. He reported that his men had captured the colors while in the process of liberating Turnbull's battery:

> Seeing the enemy in possession of three of our guns, I made a charge at the head of about 150 men and succeeded in recapturing them, taking from one the colors of the Eighth Florida regiment, and bringing in as prisoners the major of that regiment and some 30 of his men.[10]

There is a possibility that someone in the 8th Florida picked it up after having been passed over by the 19th Maine, then recaptured moments later by Sgt. Thomas Hogan, 72nd New York.[11] "I regret to state that, while retreating, the colors of the Eighth Florida Regiment were left upon the field, the color-bearer and color–guard [one sergeant and two corporals] being killed or wounded and left upon the field," wrote Colonel Lang of the flag incident. "I cannot attach any blame to the commander of this regiment, as in the confused order of the retreat several colors were crowded near each other, and the flag was not missed until the brigade was halted at the woods, too late to rescue it."[12]

As Brewster's Excelsior Brigade advanced to the left of Heath's regiment, General Carr's small line continued northwest toward Weir's guns, shifting to a right oblique and away from the 19th Maine. A gap began to form between Heath's right and Carr's left, isolating the Confederates between them. In the confusion, a number of men belonging to the 2nd Florida's center did not receive the order to retire. In the low ground and heavy growth, with all the smoke and confusion swirling about them, and the battle an incessant roar, they could not see or hear any commands directing them to withdraw. While the men crowded in the center held their position in the thickets, both flanks systematically pulled back, the right retiring west, the left shifting north toward Wright's Georgians. As Union forces pressed these flanks the men in the center became trapped.

By the time Brewster had retaken Turnbull's three guns,

Heath's regiment had reclaimed all the ground it had lost, pressing Lang well beyond Plum Run. His center remained, hopelessly trapped. Here, Colonel Heath stopped and delivered one last volley into the disorganized enemy. His men now stood perhaps 200 yards west–northwest of Turnbull's gun line. The Klingle barn was but 400 yards off. Heath rode up and down his line encouraging his men to choose their targets, take their time. To the south, the colors of the 111th New York were waving beyond the left front of Turnbull's liberated battery.

Chapter 17 | Forward To The Front

Before Hancock had repositioned Weir's battery, east of the Codori barn, he and others had sent aides riding to fetch reinforcements. The aides had done their jobs. Reinforcements were at this moment pouring onto Cemetery Ridge at an incredible rate. Brig. Gen. Henry J. Lockwood, commanding the Second Brigade, First Division, Twelfth Corps, arrived on the scene with two units, the 1st Maryland Potomac Home Brigade and the 150th New York. They advanced from near Culp's Hill over to the Taneytown Road using a small lane referred to today as Hunt Avenue. They headed south at the double-quick, then turned right where George Weikert's farm lane intersected that avenue. Then it was up the ridge, through Patterson's Woods, and out onto the crest where present day U.S. Avenue intersects Hancock Avenue.

Col. William P. Maulsby's Marylanders were in the lead, and they were directed north by the right flank. The scene on the crest of the ridge was one of massive chaos. At least four batteries, or portions there of, were parked near the George Weikert farm, units belonging to Clark, Bucklyn, Winslow, and Hart. Having survived the Peach Orchard and Wheatfield, the cannoneers were surrounded by hundreds of infantry, most notably from Caldwell's division.

Maulsby stopped just south of where Father Corby had blessed the Irish Brigade before that unit ventured south. Fronting due west, the 1st Maryland was joined by 150th New York. Patterson's Woods were to their immediate rear.

Meade sent the two units in. He had followed them, and he now directed Lockwood to advance, but not to venture as far as the Emmitsburg Road, as Sickles had done. Meade then returned to the Taneytown Road and spurred his horse north. "The First Regiment Potomac Home Brigade, Maryland Volunteers, Col. William P. Maulsby, formed the first line, and the One hundred and fiftieth New York Volunteers, Colonel Ketcham, the second line," reported Lockwood. "Thus formed, these regiments under my charge, advanced about 1 mile, a portion in double-quick amid the most terrific firing of shells and musketry, to and beyond the extreme front, driving the enemy [Barksdale] before them and entirely clearing the field."[1] Maulsby added, "On their arrival on the field of battle, they were instantly deployed in line, this regiment forming the first and One hundred and fiftieth New York the second and supporting the line of battle, and advanced and engaged the enemy."[2]

Maulsby's regiment advanced through Thompson's and Phillip's five engaged cannon. He led his men into the gap between the 125th and the 39th New York, angling toward Trostle's barn in the distance. The gunners ceased firing as his line charged past, weapons at right shoulder shift, their left flank now passing into Trostle's Lane. The 39th New York, which at that moment was east of and above Plum Run, to the rear of a stone wall, was still trading volleys with the departing 21st Mississippi, now west of it, also behind a stone wall, as the 1st Maryland closed.

Relieving the 39th along Trostle's Lane, Maulsby's line passed over that regiment, the stone wall, and Plum Run, only to come under a murderous fire from Alexander's batteries in the Peach Orchard. Pressing onward in near darkness, the 1st Maryland reached the wall that had hindered Bigelow's withdrawal west of and above the run as they pursued Colonel Humphreys's Mississippians up the crest of the Emmitsburg Road Rise. Maulsby's far right lagged a bit as it closed on the Trostle barn, taking a partial enfilade fire from a few of Barksdale's retiring troops who had sought refuge behind yet another wall north of the barn.

With the right wing north of the lane securing Trostle's farmyard, the left redressed at the wall. Alexander's gunners had a near perfect left-enfilade at less than 300 yards. This did not deter the Marylanders, as Maulsby's men surged over the wall and entered what was once the 9th Massachusetts Battery, recapturing four Napoleons overrun by the 21st Mississippi during their advance. By this time the 21st Mississippi had retired to the crest above the battery, reforming on the opposite side. Supported by infantry off his right [Wofford], and Alexander's artillery fire, Colonel Humphreys's Mississippians persuaded the 1st Maryland to go no further. Maulsby, though he had 674 men under his command, could see the futility of continuing up that open slope. He had come as far as Meade had instructed, anyway. Instead he returned to the stone wall east of and above Plum Run after detaching enough men to drag the four Napoleons back across the ravine.

Col. John H. Ketchum's 150th New York moved forward moments after the 1st Maryland. Almost instantly these 609 effectives were hit by indirect shot and shell from a section of guns posted north of the Trostle farm lane's intersection with the Emmitsburg Road. Instead of angling west–southwest, however, Ketchum moved due west, passing through Thompson's and Phillips's batteries, ending their engagement. By the time the 150th reached Plum Run, their comrades from the 125th and 126th New York had already stopped Barksdale. As the 150th emerged from the thickets, west of the ravine, north of the Trostle's barn, the infantry fight was for the most part over. They continued, however, to be harassed by indirect and sporadic fire from the section posted near the Emmitsburg Road.[3]

So horrific was the carnage in the ravine that Colonel Ketchum detached men to care for wounded before his men continued on. Once in the open above the run, his left flank linked up with Maulsby's right behind a wall north–northeast of and below Trostle's barn. Here he stopped his regiment as Barksdale's retiring line reformed to the rear of another stone wall near the crest of the Emmitsburg Road Rise. Darkness had fallen and like Lockwood, Ketchum had orders not to proceed to the rise beyond. Leaving a strong skirmish line, Maulsby withdrew back to Plum Run, realigning on the 1st Maryland, whose men had also pulled back, which largely ended the fighting on this part of the line.[4]

Col. Silas Colgrove, temporarily commanding Ruger's Third Brigade, followed Lockwood up Cemetery Ridge. Directed to Caldwell's previous position, his 1,598 effectives were placed in reserve east of the crest, thus solidifying control of the ridge. Colgrove sent skirmishers forward, his men relieving the survivors of the 125th and 126th New York regiments, who were at that time caring for wounded in the ravine and lower meadows. They did not engage. Lieutenant James's section of gun belonging to the 4th U.S., Battery K, arrived and was placed by Colonel McGilvery west of the crest in front of Colgrove's left flank, just north of Trostle's lane. The lieutenant's two Napoleons that had caused General Hancock and Colonel Heath so much grief were now the two most important artillery tubes on that part of the ridge. Once James was in position, Lt. Edwin Dow's 6th Maine was pulled back from McGilvery's line above Plum Run to align off James's right. These six guns were McGilvery's anchor, and in time became the left flank of his famous Plum Run artillery line on July Third.

Chapter 18 | Reinforcements for the Center

Eight hundred yards north of Lockwood, more Federal reinforcements were pouring onto the ridge. Col. Raymond Dana, temporarily in command of Col. Roy Stone's Second Brigade, Third Division, First Corps, led the way.[1] The 143rd, 149th, and 150th Pennsylvania, aligned from south to north in line of battle on the brow of the ridge just north of the Hummelbaugh farm lane. The three units, badly mauled on July 1, numbered less than 400 men. As they dressed, two more regiments arrived off Dana's right. The 80th New York, commanded by Col. Theodore B. Gates, and the 151st Pennsylvania, under Capt. Walter T. Owens, were detached from Col. Chapman Biddle's First Brigade. The two regiments had also suffered severely on July 1, and their combined strength now was less than 300 men.

Before the signal was given to advance, Lieutenant Sheldon's 1st New York, Battery B, with Capt. James M. Rorty at the helm, came thundering over the crest. Hancock had not forgotten Battery B. After leaving the 1st Minnesota, he had continued north, recruiting support as he rode. At some point he crossed paths with Captain Rorty, acting ordnance officer for the Second Corps, who at this time was detached from the recently disbanded 14th New York Independent Battery, portions of which had been transferred to the 1st New York. Known as the Irish Brigade Battery, these three sections had previously been deemed rogue and uncontrollable and sent to various batteries then engaged at Gettysburg. Hancock promptly sent Rorty south to find and take charge of Battery B and bring it to him.

Accompanied by his adjutant, Lt. George L. Dwight, Rorty had ridden south, passing through Patterson's Woods prior to Lockwood's arrival. He came upon Battery B straddling the old Trostle Lane, engaging from an exposed position near the George Weikert farm. Disregarding military protocol, Rorty approached Lieutenant Sheldon and demanded to take command of Battery B, on Hancock's order. When Sheldon started to protest, Lieutenant Dwight confirmed Hancock's order. Without further hesitation and without reporting to McGilvery, Rorty and Sheldon ordered the guns hitched, then told the cannoneers to mount. McGilvery later recalled watching the battery leave from a distance, and wondered what happened to it.[2]

When Battery B withdrew it left Pvt. Henry Rosegrant lying sprawled on the ground in a pool of blood, shot through the face. Rorty left five wounded men behind as he led the battery back out the farm lane to the Taneytown Road. Turning north, he guided Sheldon's four commandeered Parrott Rifles through a maze of traffic, including Lockwood's approaching brigade, to the Hummelbaugh farm lane. There he turned west, retracing the route that battery had taken when Caldwell advanced. Once atop the ridge, they turned north, heading toward what once was the gap south of the copse of trees, where Brown's battery and the 19th Maine had initially been placed.[3]

Rorty had been told to report directly to Hancock, and he knew exactly where he was going. The four 10-Pounders rumbled toward Gates's line as it formed before swinging west, passing through the 80th New York, where Rorty encountered Hancock. Wheeling about in "Reverse Trot," approximately 400 yards south of the copse of trees, Battery B unlimbered under Hancock's personal supervision. Less than a minute after unlimbering, Battery B's first rounds were sailing towards Wright's Georgians as they milled about Weir's overrun battery. Rorty opened with shrapnel, his first rounds exploding over Weir's disabled guns. This fire stopped Lang's and Wright's men from dragging Weir's guns farther than they already had, dispersing those detached for that purpose.

While Rorty saw to his battery, Gates redressed his line to the rear of the limbers, the caissons having been parked at the crest. As Hancock prepared to advance the new units, Col. Francis V. Randall, commander of the 13th Vermont Regiment, Third Brigade, Third Division, First Corps, approached. He reported that his regiment was on its way and would arrive within moments. Earlier that afternoon five of his companies, commanded by Lt. Col. William D. Munson, had been detached from the regiment to support a battery on West Cemetery Hill, east of Taneytown Road.[4] A short time later, Colonel Randall personally advanced the remaining five companies into the orchard immediately south of Zeigler's

Grove west of the road. "Soon after this, I was ordered to advance the balance of my regiment a little to the front and to the left of our former position, which brought us nearly in rear of the right of the Second Corps," he wrote. "This took me entirely out of the line occupied by the rest of our brigade, and I received no further orders from our brigade headquarters during the remainder of that day."[5]

Randall's separated wings rested close enough to each other that communication was constant and unhindered. At about 6:00 P.M. Colonel Randall received orders from General Doubleday to report to Hancock. Doubleday had been riding back to Stannard's headquarters at the Catherine Guinn farm when he crossed paths with Randall and the 13th Vermont. This was quite by chance, much like Hancock's encounter with MacDougall and his 111th New York. "At this time an officer, whom I did not know at that moment, but proved to be General Doubleday, came galloping over the hill [ridge] from General Hancock's position, and approached my regiment," recounted Randall. "After having found what regiment we were, and making a few inspiring remarks to my men, he directed me to take my regiment in the direction from which he had come, and report to General Hancock, whom I would find there and hard pressed, and said he feared he would lose his artillery or some of it before I could get there."[6]

The colonel's first item of business was to consolidate his detached wings. Once that was completed he repeated Doubleday's instruction to Colonel Munson. At that point, said Randall, "I started, riding ahead of my regiment to meet

General Hancock and find where I was needed, so as to be able to place my men in position without exposing them too long under fire."[7]

Munson, who had formed the regiment in column of divisions, led the 13th Vermont at a slight left angle up the eastern slope of the ridge toward the copse of trees. At some point he took an oblique line of march which placed him on a course due south, passing the copse of trees east of and below the crest. The regiment then angled half-right up the slope of the ridge and crested it somewhere west of Peter Frey's property.[8]

Munson spotted Colonel Randall with Hancock. "As I reached the ridge or highest ground between the cemetery and Little Round Top Mountain, I met General Hancock, who was encouraging and rallying his men to hold on to the position," wrote Munson. "He told me the rebels had captured a battery he had had there, and pointed out to me the way they had gone with it, and asked if I could retake it. I told him I could, and that I was willing to try. He told me it would be a hazardous job, and he would not order it, but if I thought I could do it, I might try."[9]

Just as with Doubleday before him, Hancock had no idea to whom he was speaking other than a colonel of infantry. Some years later, Hancock inquired, "What regiment of Vermont Troops were those I met on the evening of the second day? Reynolds I think, was in command of the regiment that drew back the guns." The "Reynolds" to whom he referred was, of course, Randall.[10]

Within moments of their conversation, the head of Randall's approaching column appeared off the 80th New York's right flank. Randall described how he aligned his regiment:

> By this time my regiment had come up, and I moved them to the front far enough so that when I deployed them in line of battle they would leave Hancock's [actually Doubleday's] men in their rear. They were now in column by divisions, and I gave the order to deploy in line, instructing each captain as to what they were to do as they came on to the line, and, taking my position to lead them, gave the order to advance.[11]

The 13th Vermont numbered 636 effectives, a few less then Gates's and Dana's five combined regiments, but they were fresh. When Randall started forward, both Gates and Dana advanced also, their combined numbers now swollen to over 1,000 muskets.[12]

While Randall formed his line, Carr's small brigade was trading musketry with the gray–clad line belonging to Maj. W. R. Moore's 2nd Florida, then isolated in the run north of the 19th Maine. The 13th Vermont came under small arms fire from this same unit as they stepped off. So minimal was this fire intended for Carr that Colonel Randall never knew of it as he ordered double–quick with arms at right–shoulder–shift.

Within minutes Carr's small numbers were absorbed into Randall's left wing as it rolled past. What organization

Carr had assembled was now utterly lost. Not to be deterred, he again rallied a few of his men, but not before Colonel Dana's two regiments passed through. Again Carr lost men in the confusion, and again Carr reorganized his rag-tag unit. In short order, Carr's small irregular line found itself skirmishing in the dark west of the Emmitsburg Road, north of the 13th Vermont and Roger's house, where Carr's withdrawal had initially begun.

Not long after the 13th Vermont stepped off, a single ball brought down Randall's horse. He was not a man easily discouraged, however, and he led the men forward on foot, descending toward Plum Run. "While on the ground, I discovered a rebel line debouching from the woods [Plum Run thickets] on our left, and forming substantially across our track about 40 rods away," wrote Randall. "We received one volley from them, which did us very little injury, when my men sprang forward with the bayonet with so much precipitancy that they appeared to be taken wholly by surprise, and threw down themselves down in the grass, surrendering, and we passed over them."[13]

Randall, of course, was unaware that Colonel Heath's 19th Maine had pushed far beyond these men, isolating them near Plum Run, where they had missed Colonel Lang's order to withdraw. Carr's appearance made things worse for them and, coupled with the additional weight of another few hundred men from Dana's line, it is no wonder the remnants of Moore's regiment surrendered en masse to Randall.

When the 13th hesitated in the run, General Hancock,

who was following Dana, spurred his horse through the lines. Riding up to Randall, he told the colonel to ignore the prisoners and "press on for the guns." The colonel responded by sending his right wing farther to the west-northwest, angling toward the Codori barn, where they overran those Confederates trying to drag away Weir's three Napoleons and retook them without a struggle.[14]

Stopping only long enough to send prisoners back through his lines, Randall quickly dressed his line and continued west with the left wing. Not hesitating at Weir's half–battery, Munson's right wing quickly caught up, leaving the three Napoleons sitting where they had been recaptured. Capt. B. C. McCurry of the 22nd Georgia wrote, "The regiment captured three pieces of cannon, but, owing to the brigade giving way on our right [2nd Florida], we were compelled to give back and abandon our captured booty."[15] That Captain McCurry was the only captain out of seven to return unscathed provides a stark measure of how badly mauled the 22nd Georgia had been. As previously mentioned, the regimental commander, Colonel Wasden, had been mortally wounded.[16]

After stopping to send several volleys toward the retiring enemy, Randall dressed the entire line and advanced toward the Emmitsburg Road. Just south of the Codori barn he could see a single cannon—a Napoleon—on the road. Randall took this to be a Confederate piece, but it was, in fact, one of Lieutenant Livingston's captured guns. Capt. Charles J. Moffett, commanding the 2nd Georgia Battalion, recalled that, "Major

Ross was wounded near the brick house while endeavoring to turn the heads of the [captured] artillery horses toward our lines."

Men from the 2nd Georgia struggled with the two unruly and possibly wounded horses while they attempted to get that gun back to their lines. It probably would have been easier to cut the horses loose and drag it back by the prolonge ropes. It has never been explained why Captain Moffett or Major Ross chose to haul that gun back using frightened and panicked animals. Either way, the tube cost the lives of several Georgians, including Ross. It was an expensive prize.

With no limber or horses to impede them, men from the 2nd Florida were having more success. They physically manhandled Livingston's second piece back by the prolonge and drag ropes, through the gate south of the barn. Once in the road they continued south toward the Rogers house where members of the 13th Vermont saw them. Believing this to be one gun of a Confederate section, Randall made ready to charge.

The first thing he did was realign his regiment to front the Roger's House to the west–southwest, his right now in the road and his left east of it, at a slight oblique. It was about this time that a hidden battery opened on his regiment from farther south on the Emmitsburg Road, nearer the Trostle lane intersection. It was probably this fire that Randall mistook as coming from Livingston's captured Napoleon only 100 yards away.

Before charging, Randall aligned his left wing with the

right, the latter having recaptured a gun (Livingston) in the road just south of the Codori farm. This put his regiment at slight left-angles to the 19th Maine and at angles to both Dana's approaching right flank, and to Carr, who was then moving up in Randall's rear. Ordering the 13th forward, Randall charged directly up the Emmitsburg Road, driving off the men dragging Livingston's remaining Napoleon. "We were now very near the Emmitsburg Road, and I advanced my line to the road, and sent my adjutant back to inform General Hancock of our position," Randall wrote. "While he was gone, the rebels advanced two pieces of artillery into the road about 100 rods to the south of us, and commenced to shell us down the road, whereupon I detached one company, and advanced them under cover of the road, dug way, and fences with instructions to charge upon and seize those guns, which they did so gallantly."[18]

Since there were no Confederate guns, sections, or batteries north of Klingle's orchard, the guns Randall was referring to must have been Livingston's section. They pushed on to the Rogers house. Randall recalled: "We also captured the rebel picket reserve, consisting of 3 officers and 80 men, who had concealed themselves in a [Rogers] house near by."[19]

Once the 13th Vermont crushed Lang's irregular line, there is nothing to indicate they encountered anything but light resistance. When Randall's right wing angled toward the Codori farm it opened a small gap in the ranks. Although the right moved due west it still, nevertheless, drifted slightly north, to close the gap This uncovered Dana's three regiments, who could now advance to the left of Randall's flank unhindered. Dana's three regiments moved into the hole between the 19th Maine's right and 13th Vermont's left, mopping up prisoners and caring for the wounded.

Dana was west of Plum Run and the 19th Maine when Randall's Vermonters charged across his front on their way to the Rogers house. Although it was near dark, Dana's line took sporadic enfilading artillery fire from the guns north of the Trostle lane. Unable to reply, Dana ordered his men to lie down in the low ground 500 yards north–northeast of the Klingle barn. He then allowed volunteers to break ranks to care for the wounded.

Having taken the Rogers house, Randall continued south toward the Klingle rise, 500 yards distant. Passing by the front of Dana's and Heath's regiments, the 13th Vermont swung half-right oblique to face west-southwest, re-occupying Turnbull's initial position immediately south of the Rogers house, west of the road. This move allowed the masked battery on the Emmitsburg Road south of them to lob solid shot down the length of Randall's line near the road. Unable to reply, Randall wisely withdrew the 13th Vermont to a position east of the road, ending hostilities on that part of the line. It was near 7:00 P.M.

Chapter 19 | Aftermath

Long before the firing had stopped along Plum Run, stretcher-bearers were already removing casualties. Starting atop the crest, they worked their way down the slope toward the ghastly ravine. They were soon joined by hundreds of infantrymen, who turned now from fighting and killing to administering to the fallen, comrade and foe alike. The scene on the crest and slope of Cemetery Ridge between the Trostle and Hummelbaugh Farm Lanes was terrible, but the carnage in Plum Run and the ravine defied description. Bodies by the hundreds lay in grotesque heaps along the entire length of the Run. From its source near the Codori barn, where Captain Moffett of the 2nd Georgia Battalion was killed while turning Livingston's gun, south to Trostle's Lane, where 2nd Lt. Adolphus Werner of Company C, 39th New York, lay shot in the chest, over one thousand men lay wounded, or dead, torn, maimed, and dismembered. Plum Run ran red with blood.

By 7:00 P.M. most of the firing between the Hummelbaugh and Trostle farm lanes had subsided. Only a few scattered rifle cracks could be heard now and again, mostly coming from the direction of Trostle's meadows, south of the Klingle house. By 8:00 P.M., even that firing had stopped. As darkness shrouded the field in a sulfurous blanket, an eerie quiet descended upon the meadows, woods, orchards, and ravines.[1] The moon rose an hour past sunset and cast a ghastly light on fields full of grotesque shapes and unrecognizable shadows.[2] More of these shadowy forms were moving than not, giving the landscape a crawling effect. Upturned staring faces caught the light. It was still and oppressively hot. Soon, lanterns appeared, followed by the jingling of ambulance wagons moving along and below the ridge. It would be a long and terrible night, not only for the wounded, but also for those charged with caring for them.

Randall's 13th Vermont lost about 30 wounded on July Second, with an additional 10 missing in action. Most of his casualties came from the masked enfilading artillery fire from the south, suffered while the regiment was west of the Emmitsburg Road. By 7:30 P.M., the 13th was winding its way back toward Cemetery Ridge after having been relieved by the 16th Vermont.

After reporting to General Doubleday, Randall placed his regiment in line of battle near the spot where Hancock had initially sent them in. On July Third, the 13th Vermont would again be called upon to advance beyond the principal line of battle. Unlike on July Second, however, when they charged a pocket with a few hundred isolated men in it, on July Third, this single regiment faced over one thousand Confederates when they advanced and then wheeled to strike Pickett's right flank. The total number of casualties sustained by the 13th Vermont on July Second was less than that suffered by any infantry regiment from either army that fought between the Hummelbaugh and Trostle farm lanes.

It is impossible to estimate how many casualties Dana's three regiments—the 143rd, 149th, and 150th Pennsylvania—suffered on July Second, so many were reported missing afterward. Certainly, most of their losses had been suffered the day before. Of the 271 reported missing in Dana's Consolidated Field Returns, most, if not all, had been captured or had disappeared on July First. There is, however, a reasonable chance that a few were killed on July Second and were never identified. According to Lieutenant Colonel Musser's report, the 143rd Pennsylvania had no casualties on July Second. However, the records indicate that Pvt. James Miles died in a Baltimore hospital on August 1, 1863, after the amputation of his left leg in a field hospital as a result of a gunshot wound received on July Second.[3]

Musser also claimed that the 143rd was responsible for retaking at least a portion of Turnbull's guns, stating that his regiment was double-quicked forward "to assist in driving back the enemy and recapturing some guns." He further stated that his regiment had held its position with the brigade near the Emmitsburg Road. "We lay upon our arms all night in line of battle." Like Colonel Musser, Capt. John Irvin, commanding the 149th Pennsylvania, reported no casualties on July Second, as did Capt. George W. Jones, commanding the 150th Pennsylvania. Captain Jones also reported that his regiment brought back two guns and caissons on the morning of July Third after spending the night near the Emmitsburg Road.[4]

The 150 men of Brewster's brigade returned to the Low

Rough Ground after being relieved by the 16th Vermont. They reformed in the small woods where they had assembled. Against orders, some started small fires to make coffee, but most did without. Instead, they wandered about in small groups, helping stretcher-bearers care for the wounded. At about midnight, Colonel Brewster finally ordered what remained of his men to lie down and get some rest.

Remarkably, by dawn almost every wounded soldier who fell between the farm lanes had been removed to a hospital. Because Brewster's dead and wounded were spread over a half-mile square area, it is impossible to be sure how many were hit during his time in the rough ground or during the succeeding counter-charge. Although the 16th Vermont had relieved them about 7:30 P.M. on the evening of July Second, Brewster did not pull the remnants of his brigade back to Cemetery Ridge until after dawn the following morning.[5]

Having squeezed into the small gap between the 19th Maine's right and the 149th Pennsylvania's left, General Carr's irregular little line settled in for a long night of picket duty along the Emmitsburg Road. With skirmishers still deployed west of it, an uneasy truce ensued during which both Federals and Confederates cared for the fallen. West of the road, most of the casualties were Confederate, while east, between the road and Plum Run, Carr's dead were strewn across the fields. "I again occupied the field I had but a few moments previously vacated," reported General Carr. "Here my command remained until morning, the officers and men assisting in removing from the field a [good] many of the wounded as the time and facilities would permit."[6] A little after dawn the following morning, Carr retired to Cemetery Ridge, but not without drawing Confederate artillery fire.[7] By 6:00 A.M., his small line was back with Humphreys's Division.

South of the 19th Maine, General Humphreys's small contingent took control of the vital rise west of Plum Run, allowing MacDougall's 111th New York to return to the ravine. After detaching men to help with the wounded, General Humphreys requested reinforcements to support his thin skirmish line, then fronting west and south. It is impossible to develop an accurate estimate of casualties, as there was no regimental organization.

General Birney responded to Humphreys's request by sending several companies of U.S. sharpshooters, detached from Col. Hiram Berdan's First Regiment. The arrival of this contingent permitted the general to pull his irregular line back from the rise to Cemetery Ridge. Humphreys's men re-crossed Plum Run over much the same ground they had counter-charged. Capt. Adolphus Cavada, one of Humphreys's staff officers, who ventured back and forth over Plum Run that evening, reported:

> On every side lay stiffened cold bodies of our dead soldiers, sometimes two or three forming ghastly groups together—in most unnatural attitudes—Sometimes lying naturally and as if asleep, occasionally a wounded man not able to move would draw our attention by plaintive moans or

a request for water. These we comforted with the assurance that the ambulances would find them in a few minutes. We found but few Rebel dead or wounded on this side [east] of the hollow, but on crossing it they became very numerous, even more so then our own.[8]

The captain also remembered the low, clinging, acrid smoke mixing with a rising mist, and that the strange musty smell peculiar to battlefields immediately after the conclusion of a fight lingered all night.

After being relieved by General Humphreys, MacDougall withdrew the 111th New York east of Plum Run, rejoining the 125th and 126th in the meadow south of Thomas's battery, where the 1st Minnesota had charged. After passing back over Plum Run north of the knoll, the colonel requested permission from Colonel Willard to see to his wounded, whom he knew to be laying but a few hundred yards south. His request was denied.

Grimly, MacDougall reformed his line as ordered. Willard would have been glad to detach men from all three of his regiments to care for the wounded if he had sufficient time and resources available to do so. As it was, he had received immediate orders to report back to General Hays. The fighting then in progress on East Cemetery Hill had drawn off three of Colonel Carroll's regiments, leaving Hays with only five to hold the Emmitsburg Road. Willard's stretcher-bearers would have to handle their task alone.

Willard started his brigade north, angling toward the front of Thomas's Napoleons, heading toward the Low Rough Ground. His three regiments traversed the gentle slope just east of the run, crossing the debris-littered field over which the 1st Minnesota had charged. The carnage was everywhere, with Union dead and wounded scattered over a wide front east of the ravine. As they neared the ravine, the bodies of casualties from the 1st Minnesota grew more and more numerous. Beyond Colvill's right flank, Confederate dead lay mangled in the ravine, rent by Thomas's double-canister. Mercifully, darkness hid the terrible sight beyond the thickets where Turnbull's demolished limbers still sat.

Passing north of Thomas, where Brewster was reforming, Willard led his "Harpers Ferry Cowards" into the Low Rough Ground. Here, as they slowly picked their way north, one of the evening's final artillery rounds exploded above the trees, carrying away half of Colonel Willard's head. He died instantly, at the very moment of his command's redemption. Colonel Sherrill, commander of the 126th New York, assumed Willard's position at the head of the column. Sherrill led his men out of the Rough Ground near where General Carr's brigade had reformed, stopping below Cemetery Ridge near the Hummelbaugh Farm Lane to close up the ranks.

MacDougall was still concerned about his wounded and approached Sherrill to request permission to send back help. His 111th New York had suffered terrible casualties—far more than either the 125th or 126th. In less then 30 minutes of combat, the 111th had sustained 185 casualties, of whom

58 had been killed or mortally wounded. During the charge into the ravine, Company A, anchoring MacDougall's right flank, sustained 33 killed and wounded, whilst the two companies to its left sustained a combined twenty-seven killed and wounded.[9]

Lt. Col. Levin Crandell, commanding the 125th New York, reported 75 casualties, sixteen of whom had been either killed or mortally wounded, with 14 missing. Colonel Sherrill's own 126th took about 100 casualties, of whom 31 were killed or mortally wounded, with an additional 10 men missing in action. Major Hildebrandt's detached 39th New York lost 21 killed or mortally wounded along the Trostle lane. One-third of his 70 casualties had been hit by artillery fire along the wall above Plum Run.[10]

A measure of the tenacity of MacDougall's 111th New York on July Second is that the returns reported not a single man captured or missing. There were many reasons for this—the regiment's superior position, its firm discipline in the most extreme circumstances, its concentrated firepower on those below, and Colonel MacDougall's calming demeanor under fire. Of the thirteen field officers who had advanced with the regiment, eleven had been shot down, leaving only Colonel MacDougall and Lt. Col. Isaac Lusk unscathed. Three officers were killed, three seriously wounded, and five slightly wounded.

Colonel Sherrill discussed the issue of the wounded with MacDougall and Crandell. Several dozen men from each regiment were detached to return south. It is not known precisely how many were sent. We do know, however, that over two hundred wounded men were recovered by dawn, including all of those belonging to Willard's brigade. Sherrill returned his brigade to its initial position at the Bryan farm. The 39th New York rejoined him there about 9:00 P.M. Because Carroll's detached regiments had been sent to East Cemetery Hill, most of Sherrill's command assumed positions to the rear of or along the wall south of the Bryan barn.

Captain Messick, commanding what was left of the 1st Minnesota, sent teams into the ravine to search for his wounded. Messick had been ordered back to Harrow's initial position, south of the copse of trees, shortly after hostilities had ceased. It is alleged that he joined one of the detachments that ventured back south, where they found a sight as terrible as Captain Cavada described. Pvt. Charles Carpenter, one of Messick's volunteers, wrote: "The ground was strewn with dead and dying whose groans and prayers and cries for help and water rent the air."[11]

The 1st Minnesota's dead and wounded extended from the brow of the ridge, where they had begun the charge, west some 300 yards to Plum Run. The volunteers examined each and every body they found. If the man was dead, they moved on. Siblings of several missing brothers made up part of this ghastly detail.[12]

As organized as the search was, many walking wounded bled to death while trying to seek help, collapsing as much as a quarter mile away from where they had been hit. Still, many others found relief. A dozen or so survivors from the 1st

Minnesota found refuge in Battery C. Pvt. Matthew Marvin had been shot in the ravine and passed over by the searchers. Although he couldn't walk, he eventually clawed his way up the rise until he reached Turnbull's position. He survived.

Though separated by the color of their uniforms, the wounded were treated alike. Cannoneers from both Thomas's and Turnbull's batteries joined Messick's men in the ravine to their front, helping the wounded and identifying the dead. Lieutenant Turnbull recalled that his men counted more Confederate dead and wounded than Federals, demonstrating the deadliness of Thomas's double-canister. Turnbull also remembered carrying dozens of wounded Confederates into the Low Rough Ground, where a temporary disposition staging area had been established. From here, ambulances and stretcher-bearers carried their wards to designated hospitals.[13]

Men of the 1st Minnesota carried one unidentified Alabaman, his left arm shattered, back to Thomas's battery. As with Private Marvin, Thomas's men made sure the critically wounded Johnnie was ministered to before sending him to a hospital. Pvt. Patrick Taylor, searching for his missing brother, Isaac, found his critically wounded commanding officer instead. He called immediately for help, then he and some buddies carried Colonel Colvill all the way back to the Nathaniel Lightner farm, a distance of over one mile. Colvill survived.[14]

Private Carpenter remembered their duty that night with a shudder: "In the darkness we hurried, stumbling over the field searching for our fallen companions, and when our living were cared for, laid ourselves down on the ground to gain a little rest." By 10:00 P.M., all of their wounded had been removed from the field, and most of the dead were accounted for. Those still missing and presumed dead would have to wait until July Third to be accounted for. As with MacDougall's 111th New York, Captain Messick reported no one captured or missing.[15]

At some point between 10:00 P.M. and midnight, with the night's grisly work behind them, Captain Messick finally assembled his survivors and took roll. Approximately 50 men answered his call—hardly enough to make up a good company. By 1:00 A.M., he and most of his men were sound asleep under a shining moon. Within an hour, however, clouds rolled in, bringing a passing shower, which apparently failed to wake them. By 4:00 A.M. some of Messick's men had returned to the ravine to continue their search. Sadly, they found nothing but corpses. By 6:00 A.M. on July Third, the survivors of the 1st Minnesota had been fed and watered, and were back with Harrow's brigade near the copse of trees.

Colonel Heath led the 19th Maine back toward Plum Run after pickets belonging to the 16th Vermont relieved them. Colonel Brewster did not argue when Heath stopped to collect Turnbull's guns. Hauling back the three trophies, the 19th crossed Plum Run for the fourth time that day. They continued up Cemetery Ridge, traversing the same ground they had earlier contested. Cheers from the men of Doubleday's division greeted them near the ridge. "When the Regiment returned to its former position, it took back three twelve-pounders [brass] which it had recaptured, and four caissons. When we reached the place from which we had charged, we found a new line of battle, made up of new troops from other corps," remembered Sergeant Adams. "When the regiment appeared upon the scene with the three guns and four caissons coming from the direction of the enemy, the whole line went wild with cheers over the brilliant charge and capture by the Nineteenth Maine."[16] He continued. "While elated by our success in repulsing the enemy, it was a very sad night to most of the boys of the regiment."[17]

Heath lost 38 soldiers killed or mortally wounded, while another 70 received lesser wounds, and four were missing. The 19th Maine lost approximately one-third of its effective fighting capacity in less than one hour. "When the roll was called, many a brave boy for the first time failed to respond to his name. The answers made by the living for their dead or wounded comrades were pathetic," wrote John Smith. "As the names of the missing would be called, such answers as these would be returned: 'John was killed before we fired a shot.' 'I saw Frank throw up his arms and fall just after we fired the first volley.' 'Jim was shot through the head.' 'Charley was killed while we were charging across the plain this side of the brick [Codori] house."[18] Unlike the survivors from 1st Minnesota who reportedly slept soundly that night, many in the 19th Maine could not close their eyes.

Like most of the other regimental commanders, Colonel Heath detailed men from the 19th to help search for wounded. His men labored long into the night, bringing back casualties from both armies. In the bitter process they passed over many a wounded man, leaving those unfortunate wretches too badly torn to be moved to suffer an agonizing and lonely death. By 11:00 P.M., all of the 19th's wounded had been removed, and Heath's men were back on Cemetery Ridge. "The boys of the Nineteenth lay down upon the ground to rest for the night at nearly the point from which we charged in the late afternoon," recalled Smith. "There was not much sleep that night. The cries of the wounded men, lying between the lines, suffering from pain and burning with fever were most pitiful."[19]

The following morning Heath's men awoke to a scene unlike any they would see again until Cold Harbor. Hundreds of bloated bodies littered the landscape, their glazed eyes staring unflinching toward the heavens. The dead lay scattered almost as far as the eye could see, strewn across the plain over which Heath's column had charged. Most were on their backs, having been turned that way the night before.

After sending four companies to the skirmish line that morning, Heath saw to it that his ammunition and several cases of hardtack were distributed. He then sat down to eat his first meal in nearly 24 hours, and wondered what would come next.

Captain Dunbar Ransom, wounded while at Turnbull's battery's forward-most position, reported to a field hospital to have his wound examined. The surgeons probed the wound, extracted the ball, dressed, and bandaged the wound, then sent him on his way. After a night's rest and cup of coffee the captain reported for duty to General Tyler.

Chapter 20 | After Thoughts

Twelve organized Federal regiments engaged along Plum Run between the Hummelbaugh Farm and Trostle Farm Lanes on July Second, while portions of at least thirteen others supported them. In all, 25 regiments in one form or another participated in the attack and repulse of 12 Confederate regiments. From left to right, beginning on the Old Trostle Lane and extending north to the Hummelbaugh Lane, a distance of approximately 1,050 yards, the organized Federal regiments were the 39th, 125th, 126th, and 111th New York, 19th Massachusetts, 42nd New York, 1st Minnesota, 19th Maine, 143rd, 149th, and 150th Pennsylvania, and the 13th Vermont.

There is no way to be sure how many men from Stone's [Dana's][1] brigade participated in the day's fighting, as the numbers do not exist. A rough estimate can be made based on the following: if Stone lost sixty percent of his effective strength July First, as was reported, this left Dana with roughly 530 men. Dana's participation was secondary—his three small regiments trailed behind the line that broke the Confederates. Although their weight was not felt in the counter-attack, their contribution was not without value. When they descended into Plum Run, they scooped up nearly one-quarter their total number in prisoners. Excluding Dana's 530 men, the remaining nine organized regiments numbered approximately 3,475 effectives.

The thirteen partial regiments that faced back did so in three separate and irregular lines. While these lines included men from many different units, they still managed to retain a semblance of coherence, as defined by the colors of the various regiments. On the left, General Humphreys's line displayed colors from the 16th Massachusetts, 12th New Hampshire, 12th New Jersey, and 26th Pennsylvania, in all numbering approximately 300 rifles. North of Humphreys position, Brewster's 150 men came from his own 70th, 71st, 72nd, 74th, and 120th New York regiments, with, no doubt, a few others who turned and stood with them. Carr's 100 rifles came not only from the regiments named above, but also from the 105th Pennsylvania. Although there were men from other units who participated, the colors on the field represented these regiments. The exact number of those who faced back will never be known, but as suggested above, a reasonable estimate is a little over 500 men.

Thirty-seven artillery pieces, drawn from seven different batteries, were on hand to lend support to the counterattack, after Plum Run had been reached. It is hard to derive an exact number engaged, as it is possible some may not have opened. Again, from left to right, beginning near the Old Trostle Lane, they were the 1st New York, Battery B [Sheldon-Rorty]–four 10-pounder Parrotts, 5th U.S. Battery I [Watson]–four 10 pounder Parrots, 6th Maine Light [Dow]–four 12-pounder Napoleons, 5th Massachusetts [Phillips]–three Ordnance Rifles, 1st Pennsylvania, Battery C [Thompson]–two Ordnance Rifles, 4th U.S., Battery C [Thomas]–six Napoleons, 3rd U.S.

Batteries F & K, Consolidated–six Napoleons, 4th U.S., Battery K–two Napoleons [Seeley–James], and 5th U.S., Battery C [Weir]–six Napoleons. It is likewise impossible to determine accurately the number of artillerymen who helped to stop the Confederate advance. However, these men brought their combined firepower to bear, and made a large contribution to the repulse of the Rebel assaults.

Watson's regulars had been placed in a precarious position. The lieutenant's primary job was to stop the advancing 21st Mississippi who had, on his arrival, just overrun Bigelow's 9th Massachusetts Light, west of and above the run. Watson's four rifles were the last organized unit along the length of Trostle's lane from the ravine east to Patterson's Woods. His small doses of canister failed to do much damage to the closing ranks of Confederates once Colonel Humphrey's Mississippians crossed over the wall west of the run. The ravine too proved to be a problem for Watson. Unable to depress his tubes to train into the run, he watched helplessly as Humphreys's redressed lines surged out of the ravine only 100 yards west of him, too many to contend with. When musketry poured into Battery I's left flank from Trostle Woods [Wofford] it was over. Watson did, however, hold on long enough for the 1st New York Battery B to unlimber to its rear. Like Bigelow, Watson had held at all costs. Although he was posted just south of the Trostle farm lane, we include Watson in our story, as his stand was the beginning of the end of the Confederate advance.

Although the 1st New York's engagement was brief, it

was the first battery to open on the 21st Mississippi after it had overrun Watson's 5th U.S., Battery I, east of and above Plum Run, just south of Trostle's Lane, stopping Colonel Humphreys's advance. Its fire also convinced men in Wofford's brigade, who had penetrated the Trostle Woods as far east as George Weikert's Farm, to stay south of the stone wall separating them from Trostle's lane. Had that brigade, or portions of it, swung north, to reinforce the 21st Mississippi when the issue hung in the balance, there is no telling what might have occurred.

The 6th Maine Light battery joined Battery B moments after the latter opened. Very shortly thereafter, the 39th New York Infantry charged past both batteries, driving back the 21st Mississippi and recovering all four of Watson's Parrotts.[2] The combined five Ordnance Rifles of the 5th Massachusetts and 1st Pennsylvania helped check Barksdale's already battered right flank as it brushed past them, heading toward its showdown with Willard's 125th and 126th New York regiments, but it never stopped them. All five were able to fire into the ravine, catching portions of the 17th and 13th Mississippi regiments at slight right enfilade. When Barksdale's line withdrew, Thompson's and Phillip's gunners raked the Confederates as they retired back across Trostle's Meadows, blasting away with shell and shrapnel in the waning light, falling silent only after the 1st Maryland and 150th New York had passed through.

Turnbull's struggle west of the ravine cost Wilcox and Lang not only in casualties, but also in precious time. Although his position was overrun, the lieutenant's point-blank blasts of canister and hand-to-hand engagement stopped a portion of Wilcox's line long enough for hundreds of Federals to make good their escape. Detaching men from Wilcox's line to pull Trumbull's captured guns out diminished their effective strength as well, while others headed due north toward the red barn to attend to Lieutenant Livingston's section. Their efforts to secure the prizes were for naught, and many became casualties or prisoners themselves. As badly as Turnbull's battery had been damaged, two of its guns were deployed east of the Angle on July Third, and participated in the repulse of Pickett's Charge.

Lieutenant Weir's 5th U.S., Battery C, was the first unit General Hancock moved forward to stem the Confederate tide. Weir's devastating enfilade fire with bounding solid shot along the length of the advancing 2nd Florida forced Lang to change front. One can only speculate as to what Lang might have accomplished had he continued due east unopposed. Weir's fire split the 2nd Florida, causing large numbers of that regiment to stall, become disoriented, and finally, become so isolated that many were captured. Although shifted from his initial position, Weir held as commanded by the general—until the last.

Lieutenant James reopened from north of the "Low Rough Ground," but his participation was too brief to be effective. There is not enough documentation of the 4th U.S., Battery K's engagement on this part of the line to suggest anything more than that it engaged. Lieutenant Seeley's heroic stand at the Klingle farm far overshadowed James's misadventures along Plum Run and also his poor handling of his section before Captain Irish commandeered it. Of all the batteries that participated in slowing the Confederate advance and supporting the counter-charge, Lieutenant James's participation must be considered the least effective.

The performance of the 4th U.S., Battery C, stands in sharp contrast to James's antics. Lieutenant Thomas's steadiness under fire was remarkable and widely noted. His men discharged 450 rounds of fixed case, shell, solid shot, and canister into Wilcox and Lang's ranks in about thirty minutes, an average of 2.5 rounds per gun per minute. A well-drilled regular battery might average 3.0 rounds per minute under ideal conditions, but Thomas's situation was extreme, and there were times when his gunners held their fire for fear of hitting their own men. General Harrow, whose brigade supplied the 1st Minnesota and 19th Maine, wrote surprisingly little about his regiments, opting instead to recognize Thomas. "It would be unjust to a young and accomplished officer, Lieutenant Thomas, not to bear testimony here to his gallantry, and to credit him with destroying large numbers of the enemy by the very effective fire from his guns," wrote Harrow. "His exertions contributed largely to checking and finally repulsing the enemy at this point."[3] The "point" referred to by Harrow is the same point at which many romantics have credited the 1st Minnesota, alone, with saving the Army of the Potomac from total annihilation on July Second. Hancock also noted Thomas's performance: "In addition to the troops specially mentioned heretofore as being on the line of the Second Corps on July Second, I would mention Battery C, Fourth U.S. Artillery, commanded by Lieut. Evan Thomas. This officer is particularly mentioned for bravery and good conduct."[4]

The fire from Thomas's guns shredded the thickets to their front, destroying one of Turnbull's 12-pounders, tearing apart its gun carriage with solid shot, case, and canister. The mangled bodies of Confederate dead lay in heaps in the Plum Run ravine below it, presenting bloody evidence of why the 1st Minnesota's right flank was never enveloped from the north. When Hancock selected Thomas's position, his first thought was to cover the Hummelbaugh Farm Lane. It turned out that he had chosen very possibly the finest artillery platform on that portion of the field that day, but it was the performance of the young lieutenant and his men that made it so. As with Weir, Thomas had requested infantry support, and Hancock delivered it. Without that request, Hancock may well have never sent the 1st Minnesota south.

However well the cannoneers and artillery officers performed, the role of the artillerists was secondary to that of the infantrymen. The batteries alone, no matter how many, could not have held that line.[5] It was Union infantry, supported by artillery, that stopped the Confederate advance. Their well-placed volleys, some delivered at ranges of less than one rod, fixed bayonets, and willingness to rally and face back after having been routed displayed a tenacity that was evident for the first time in months.

When Hancock rode back to fetch the 19th Maine, other subalterns had long been in motion. Having witnessed the collapse on the left, officers of various ranks were hurrying to round up reinforcements with an efficiency never witnessed in the Army of the Potomac before. Young Third Corps lieutenants, adjutants, were commandeering artillery carriages no matter to whom they belonged. Aides and volunteers were hurrying up the Taneytown Road accosting any and all officers of rank to send help. All understood what was needed: reinforcing shock troops that would smash the enemy advance instead of waiting to be attacked.

No one understood what was needed better than Col. Edward Warner, Hunt's chief of staff and acting inspector general of artillery. He and Colonel McGilvery improvised a plan to buy time until reinforcements arrived. On orders from Hunt, he spent the entire afternoon sending battery after battery into exposed places to gain an advantage in time, no matter how little time that advantage might gain. Sacrificing men and guns was not the issue. Holding Cemetery Ridge and the Taneytown Road was. Along with Warner, McGilvery had begun assembling a line of artillery, long before Barksdale made his appearance north and east of the Peach Orchard. Forming an irregular line with his guns as quickly as they arrived, he began assembling the shock troops that would be the first to slow the advance. Case in point–they moved forward to meet and contest the enemy; they did not sit back and wait. When Warner rode north from Trostle's Lane, seeking artillery, he accidentally ran into the 1st New York, Battery B. While In the process of shifting Sheldon several hundred yards south, he probably saw Colonel Willard's approach from afar. It was possibly Warner who approached Willard and apprised him of the dire circumstances. It is known that Warner was the officer who initially requested the use of a regiment to help secure the Trostle Lane.[6]

Detached further left, the 39th New York was already moving south when Lt. Sam Peeples, a section commander in Watson's 5th U.S. Battery I, was approached while standing on a rock with arms folded across chest, his eyes fixed on the overrun battery. Peeples requested help from Colonel Hildebrandt's men in retaking the captured battery, and the 39th New York readily obliged. Hildebrandt formed his line of battle on the crest while Dow's 6th Maine Light wheeled about in "Reverse Trot" north of the Sheldon and the lane. Within a few moments, Dow's battery had opened on Watson's captured guns, and the 39th had moved to the brow of the hill. On Hildebrandt's command, his Garibaldi Guards unloosed a ferocious volley into the 21st Mississippi from a distance of less than 100 yards. By this time, a number of artillery pieces off the 39th's left were pouring canister into the disabled battery as well.

Hildebrandt saw the Mississippi line wavering below him, and ordered his men forward. The 39th New York let out a rousing "Remember Harpers Ferry," and charged. Lieutenant Peeples, brandishing a musket he scooped up from the ground, accompanied the charge of the New Yorkers. The cannons of Dow's 6th Maine and Battery B ceased fire as the 39th advanced in front of them, their colors snapping in front of the guns. To the north, the men of Willard's remaining three regiments heard the cry and looked south, almost as one.

The shock troops were advancing; the counter-attack had begun. The charge drove back the Confederate line and re-took the guns. Colonel Humphreys of the 21st Mississippi later stated that he had already ordered his regiment to retire when the 39th began its charge. Whether this claim was valid or vanity, there is no question that Hildebrandt's men confronted an already battle-weary regiment that had fought its way north under conditions many regiments could not have endured.

Excluding Dana's 530 men, approximately 3,500 Federal infantry participated in the counter-attack, engaging something less than 4,000 Confederates. The latter number is derived from the combined battle strength of Barksdale, Wilcox, and Lang, numbering 4,088 men at the beginning of their advance. Certainly their combined regiments sustained more than 88 combined casualties by the time the 19th Maine charged. The Confederate line may have numbered less than 3,500 by the time it reached Plum Run, meaning that the two sides fielded nearly equal numbers.

Numbers alone are not the story, however. Barksdale's four regiments had advanced three-quarters of a mile, from near the Millerstown Road—under a grueling fire and in severe heat—fighting sometimes hand-to-hand and uphill, for much of the way. They had already marched several miles in heat and dust, including Longstreet's infamous countermarch, just to reach their jumping-off point, and fatigue had exacted a heavy toll. North of Barksdale, Wilcox's and Lang's eight combined regiments first encountered small arms fire from Berdan's sharpshooters and the 3rd Maine, and were then subjected to artillery fire as they advanced to the stone wall and their jumping-off point. Assuredly, the Confederate ranks had already been diminished.

Between the fatigue, heat, skirmishing, sharpshooting, and sporadic artillery fire, there is no way to determine how many casualties the Confederates sustained prior to reaching Plum Run. Their dead and wounded lay sprawled between their flanks stretching from the Millerstown Road north through the Peach Orchard along the Emmitsburg Road, and beyond the Rogers House. That they advanced as far to the east as Plum Run was a feat in itself; penetrating to and holding Cemetery Ridge was quite another issue. Even the gallant Barksdale, whose brigade crashed through the Sherfy farm, fell mortally wounded near Plum Run while attempting to rally his fatigued and faltering men. Cemetery Ridge was a formable position to assail.

All twelve Confederate regiments were close to being played out by the time they reached Plum Run ravine. This, however, does not mean that the portion of Cemetery Ridge lying between the farm lanes was always secure. It was not. They had broken the Union line. Sickles's Third Corps had been driven back in disarray. On Cemetery Ridge, the Union line was taken apart piecemeal and the artillery reserve depleted in the attempt to halt the attack, and almost none of

Hancock's units were in their originally assigned positions. Caldwell's division of the Second Corps, originally the left wing of Hancock's position, opened a huge gap on the ridge when it was sent south of Hummelbaugh Farm Lane. Under normal circumstances Hancock, and any other corps commander, would not have divided his charge in the face of the enemy. He had, however, but little choice. Sending his number one division further south to support Sickles in the Wheatfield was but part of it, and is a prelude to our story.

The Federal shock troops that advanced to stop Barksdale and Wilcox broke the Confederate momentum through grit, good timing, and mutual support. Confederate and Federal units performed nobly, with the 21st Mississippi, 2nd Florida, 1st Minnesota and 111th New York, most notable among them. Hancock's direct order sent both Federal regiments into battle, and both advanced into the same pocket that became the point of the Confederate thrust. The 21st Mississippi and 2nd Florida were both isolated but fought on and advanced until they could go no farther. Once east of the Emmitsburg Road, the odds were stacked against both regiments.

Barksdale's approach from the south was doomed when Willard's three regiments north of the 39th hit him in the ravine at a slight right angle, folding him back like a jack-knife. Uneasiness within his crowded ranks turned to panic, confusion, chaos, and disorientation. His Mississippians had nowhere to go but back toward Seminary Ridge. Wilcox, on the other hand, drove forward, his regiments gaining strength as they became compressed east of the Klingle farm. The angle of his approach, combined with the contours of the terrain, placed him in this position. There were no shock troops here to meet him, just Union troops retiring. The 19th Massachusetts and 42nd New York, which were the only organized resistance available to meet the threat, failed miserably as shock troops. Sent south for just such a purpose, they waited, then retired after only two volleys. Thomas's guns are not considered as shock troops because they waited in a fixed defensive position.

Although all of the Union regiments herein mentioned contributed, some gave more than others. While the single volley let loose by the 19th Massachusetts and the 42nd New York did little more than guarantee their escape, it was, nevertheless, a volley delivered. The timing was so close on this day that even this small delay may have been fatal to the Confederate advance. Once Willard's 39th, 125th, and 126th New York Regiments made contact with Barksdale and stalled his advance, the gate to Cemetery Ridge became the ravine between the knoll, west of the run, and the "Low Rough Ground." The key to splitting the Federal Army on Cemetery Ridge on July Second lay in Wilcox's hands. At no other time during that day's battle, or even on July Third, was a portion of Cemetery Ridge—and the Taneytown Road beyond—more open for the taking.

When the men of the 111th New York hit Wilcox's right flank from above, they did irreparable damage, stopping it, and then folding it up. The impact of their assault drove in Wilcox's flank, and as the Alabamans crowded northward, there was so much confusion in the right wing that it lost its eastward thrust. Instead of being attackers driving through a huge opening in the Union line, they became defenders. From atop the knoll and south of the dry wash, MacDougall's line pumped volley after volley into Wilcox's thinning ranks. Within about ten minutes, Wilcox's line began to waver. A trickle became a stream, and a stream became a torrent of wounded and just plain tired Alabamans beating an earnest retreat back over the rise to the west. No order pulled them back—they were already getting out just as MacDougall counter-charged.

By the time the 1st Minnesota discharged their first volley into Plum Run, they had been whittled down to one half their original strength. Colvill's first volley did exactly what MacDougall's had done—it slowed Wilcox down. Colvill's second volley stopped Wilcox cold, and then the initiative lay with the 1st Minnesota. Although Wilcox's eastward momentum was lost, his compressed line east of the ravine held on until Colvill's tenacious veterans leveled their muskets and counter-charged. By the time the 1st Minnesota reached the edge of the ravine, those men of Wilcox's command still in it had become trapped. Firing into Plum Run at point blank range, Colvill's men shot down Confederates in droves while the survivors fought like hell to get out. The confusion turned to near pandemonium as too many panicky men tried to get away at once.

Taking advantage of the situation, Colvill's men swept into the ravine. Unlike MacDougall, who continued across,

Colvill was stopped—becoming trapped there himself. There
were just too many Confederates west of the run for him to
continue. The 1st Minnesota's charge had halted Wilcox, and
the tables had now turned. The moment Wilcox's men settled
down above the 1st Minnesota all was lost for both. Neither
Colvill nor Wilcox had the men to engage in a methodical
and personal slugfest between the units. Given time, Union
reinforcements would overwhelm the position, if Colvill
did not run out of men or ammunition first. To be sure, the
charge of the 1st Minnesota stopped the Confederate advance
where—and when—it mattered most. Sent to support and
defend, Colvill's Red Wings were the ultimate shock troops.

Although history has been kind to Colvill and his men,
and they deserve all of the credit they received, it has not fairly
apportioned credit to other units on this part of the line that
day. Veterans of the 1st Minnesota wrote of past deeds, their
words captured the public imagination, and they were heralded long into the next century. Lieutenant Thomas, on the
other hand, wrote little about his actions at Gettysburg—he
was a Regular Army officer merely doing his job. The veterans
of the 111th New York penned a few words but they did not
find themselves covered with glory like the 1st Minnesota.
Colonel MacDougall found other things to occupy him after the war, leaving the past to forge a future—the successful
banker was elected to Congress in 1873.

The fact is: the 1st Minnesota did not charge alone.
Without the help of Thomas's battery to guard its flank, and
the charge of the 111th New York on its left, it would have

been overrun. The 111th New York not only helped stop Wilcox and a portion of Barksdale's force, it also cleared a portion of the 1st Minnesota's left front. After all is said and done, the 111th was the second regiment to hit Wilcox, the first being the 126th New York.

The 111th New York lost more men killed or mortally wounded that day than any other regiment on any portion of the field, including the 1st Minnesota. The 111th New York ranks third overall in total Federal soldiers killed at Gettysburg while the 1st Minnesota is seventh. The 111th ranks third in total wounded, while the 1st Minnesota ranks fifth. The 111th ranks ninth in total overall casualties, with the 1st Minnesota following at fifteenth. The 1st Minnesota, because it had fewer men, lost a higher percentage of its force—sixty-seven percent—than the 111th New York, which lost sixty-three percent.

Forget the numbers. There is glory enough for all. Colonel Heath's 19th Maine's initial advance relieved pressure from Carr's retiring line, allowing portions of that brigade to reform to his rear. Heath bought time for Hancock when his men stood shoulder-to-shoulder, battling Lang and Wilcox for possession of Turnbull's Napoleons. These precious few minutes allowed Hancock sufficient time to round up support from the likes of Thomas, Colvill, Humphreys, and MacDougall. Heath also provided Colonel Brewster with the time he needed to reform portions of his shattered Excelsior brigade in the Low Rough Ground. Although Heath's second counter-charge may not have been quite as critical as that by the

1st Minnesota or the 111th New York, it broke the back of Lang's Floridians once and for all, leaving the Florida brigade largely useless on July Third.

These three Second Corps regiments did not fight alone. The 13th Vermont and the 143rd, 149th and 150th Pennsylvania regiments made critical contributions, although not, perhaps, to the level of Colvill's, MacDougall's, or Heath's, men. Humphrey's 300 men relieved the shattered 1st Minnesota and 111th New York. His men secured the rise west of Plum Run, denying the Confederates a superb artillery platform from which to enfilade North Cemetery Ridge and Hill. Brewster's role is secondary in that his line advanced in the rear of the 19th Maine, hauling in trophies and prizes earned by another regiment. Their presence in the "Low Rough Ground," however, gave weight to the rebuilding Union position, meaning that they could keep the Confederates out. Brewster's small line successfully held a very important piece of real estate.

General Carr was something of the odd man out. He was busy all over the Ridge, rallying troops and patching together an impromptu and irregular line consisting of men belonging to different brigades, divisions, even corps. He has received little credit for this work. Although his line may not have been the deciding factor, it served as a police force of a sort, rounding up prisoners and sending stragglers back to the front. In the end, his small line reclaimed all that it had lost when he sent skirmishers across the Emmitsburg Road to the positions they had initially occupied.

Hancock's hand stitched together the line. He sent in

Lieutenants Weir and Thomas, and Colonels Heath, Mac-Dougall and Colvill, either pointing the way himself, or by taking a soldier by the shoulder and placing him in line. In several instances, he was but a few yards from the enemy. Credit for saving that portion of Cemetery Ridge and securing the Taneytown Road belongs to Hancock. His men were not at the right place at the right time by accident. Under extreme pressure, the general maintained his sense of battlefield values and common sense. He knew Lieutenant Weir could not hold his position alone, promised support, and then went and got it. He repeated this feat over and over again, sending in regiments, companies, squads, groups, and even single men. When he placed his hand on a man or called out to a unit, that man or that unit responded. His presence between the Hummelbaugh and Trostle farm lanes on the evening of July Second was every bit as impressive as his commanding figure was on East Cemetery Hill the evening of July First. Many men and many units fought well and nobly on July Second, but if any one man is to be called the savior of the Army of the Potomac, it is Hancock the Superb.

Epilogue

Let us return to the question of which regiment Hancock was referring to in his circular. Was it the 1st Minnesota? In an exquisite article entitled *The First Minnesota at Gettysburg,* Professor Robert W. Meinhard wrote:

> After trying to rally some of Humphreys's retreating forces, Hancock realized that the only additional men readily available were the 262 men of the First Minnesota. He cried out in despair to Colonel Colvill, "My God, are these all the men we have here"[1]

Professor Meinhard also emphasized that there are several conflicting accounts concerning the exchange, the most popular having Hancock ride up to Colvill and inquire, "What regiment is this?" with Colvill responding, "First Minnesota, sir!" As suggested by Meinhard, if this is the case, then why did Hancock issue the circular asking for identification of the regiment?[2]

In his monumental work, The Gettysburg Campaign, A Study in Command, Edwin B. Coddington describes the same excited Hancock, saying, "he roared, 'advance colonel, and take those colors,'" indicating one of Wilcox's Alabama regimental battle flags.³ It has been suggested that Hancock did not know Colvill because he did not address him by name, but the failure to address Colvill by his first or last name does not indicate or even suggest that Hancock did not know the colonel.

Even to this day, military protocol requires professional recognition by rank, especially when addressing a subordinate officer in front of enlisted personnel. What is strange about both accounts, however, is that neither suggests the direction from which Hancock approached the 1st Minnesota. It's easy to visualize the general gallantly riding down present-day Hancock Avenue from the direction of the Copse of Trees, his towering figure impressing all as he passes, his young aide trailing behind with his personal battle flag. The fact is, however, that Hancock approached Colonel Colvill and the 1st Minnesota from the south, or opposite direction, having already ordered the 111th New York Volunteer Regiment forward. Because the 111th New York belonged to Hancock's own Third Brigade, Third Division, Second Corps, one might expect that the general would be familiar with that regiment. This, however, was not the case.

The 1st Minnesota had been in the Second Corps of the Army of the Potomac almost since the beginning. William Colvill, its commander at the time of Gettysburg, had been with the regiment since its muster. He was an imposing officer, standing a towering six feet five inches tall, the kind of figure Hancock would not have easily forgotten.

The 33-year-old attorney turned newspaper editor was a natural leader and a striking figure, adored by his men and known to many. Enlisting with the 1st Minnesota upon its organization, April 29th, 1861, Colvill was officially commissioned Captain of Company F. Like most of his 399 men at Gettysburg, Colvill was a tested veteran of First Bull Run, the Seven Days Battles, Antietam, Fredericksburg, and Chancellorsville. Wounded at the Battle of Glendale, June 30, 1862, Colvill returned to the regiment a Brevet Major. By winter's end, he was brevetted lieutenant colonel and on May 6, 1863, several days after the Battle at Chancellorsville, he was commissioned colonel of the 1st Minnesota, its fifth commanding officer in two years.[4] Put simply, he was a physically imposing man who had performed extensive and distinguished service with the Army of the Potomac. Hancock knew who Colvill was—and he knew the 1st Minnesota.

On the other hand, Col. Clinton Dugland MacDougall, commander of the 111th New York, was slight of build with no striking physical characteristics, and was only 24 years old. Like Colvill, he had been wounded in battle. Unlike Colvill, however, MacDougall's slight wound did not alter the fact that he had been labeled a coward. This unspeakable dishonor occurred when the 111th New York surrendered with the entire brigade and garrison at Harpers Ferry in September 1862. Willard's Third Brigade, known as "The Harpers Ferry Cowards," had just recently returned to the field. They had joined Hancock's Second Corps at Gum Springs, only a week before, on June 25th, fresh from the defenses of Washington, D.C. A review of the available correspondence and reports, dated June 25th through July 2nd, does not indicate any reason why Hancock would have become familiar with either MacDougall or the 111th New York. While it is possible that Hancock wanted nothing to do with Willard's "Harpers Ferry Cowards," it is more likely that, in the intensity of the march north in pursuit of Lee's army, he simply had other things on his mind. The 111th would have been to him just another New York regiment—and a brand new one at that. Hancock was not familiar with either the 111th or MacDougall, which may well explain the confusion over the identity of the regiment.

MacDougall was an educated young man and an established banker by the age of 21. He served a one-term stint in Congress as a representative from upstate New York. He enlisted in the 75th New York Volunteer Infantry as a captain in early 1862, resigning that commission to accept a commission as a lieutenant colonel in the newly raised 111th New York on August 20 of that year. A no-nonsense commander, he was much like Colvill in the sense that he asked nothing of his men that he did not ask of himself. Since his parole the past September, he had held the redemption of his honor and of his regiment to be of paramount importance, and he had instilled this in his men. He knew nothing of Hancock save the rumors he had heard from many, that the general was fair yet aggressive, and all too unforgiving. As MacDougall led his men toward Gettysburg, there is nothing to indicate he had ever been introduced or presented to Hancock.[5]

Another indication that Hancock would have been familiar with Colvill is the fact his adjutant general, Col. Charles Morgan, had Colvill arrested on that same march northward.

In the words of Edwin Coddington, "Hancock had deprived him [Colvill] of his command on June 29th because he permitted his men to cross the Monocacy Creek on a log instead of wading and had thus slowed up their march."[6] Brig. Gen. John Gibbon, commanding the Second Division, Second Corps, was actually the one who filed the charges. Colvill had, over the past three days, petitioned his commanding officer, Brig. Gen. William Harrow, First Brigade, Second Division, pleading with him to intercede on his behalf. It is still uncertain at what time of day on July Second Gibbon saw to it that he was formally reinstated, if he ever did.

Still another reason why Hancock would have recognized the 1st Minnesota is that he had dealt with it several times on July Second, moving it south at one point and ordering it to stem the flight of Third Corps fugitives on another. He had no occasion to address the 111th New York directly until the moment when he ordered it forward.

The most compelling reason of all why Hancock would not have known the identity of this unit, however, was that the brigade was without battle and corps flags to designate it! Only a week earlier, it had been assigned to the Washington, D.C. defenses and had marched to join the Army of the Potomac without them.[7]

There are ample reasons why Hancock would have been familiar with Colvill and the 1st Minnesota, and few if any reasons why he would have known the 111th New York. With this in mind, it would appear that the circular of July 7 was issued to identify and give recognition to the 111th New York.

Appendix:
The Ground

Plum Run's source is an oozing underground spring located some 200 yards south of Nathaniel Codori's large farmyard, near the base of an elongated rise paralleling the Emmitsburg Road (often referred to as the Emmitsburg Road Rise). Flowing easterly toward Cemetery Ridge it widens into a shallow muddy creek as it bends south-southeast 400 yards from its source. Plum Run's principle function is that of catch, or drainage basin, for the expansive meadows located between the Emmitsburg Road and Cemetery Ridge, capturing excessive runoff for two miles as it flows south. From the base of Cemetery Ridge, at a point directly west of and below today's Hancock and Pleasonton Avenues intersection the meadow is about 900 yards wide, and is often referred to by scholars as the Broad Open Plain.

Today's ground does not fully reflect the terrain over which the battle raged on July Second, 1863, having been dramatically altered over a period of years.[1] The worst degradation began in May 1917, when Camp Colt opened as the United States Army's premier tank proving and training center. The ground over which the battle raged east of Emmitsburg Road housed hundreds of Doughboys in tent bivouacs, complete with two large mess halls, dozens of trench latrines, officers' quarters, parade grounds, showers, stables, quartermaster and commissary buildings, and, several maintenance garages.[2]

Meandering through the Broad Open Plain east of the Klingle farm, Plum Run widens to about ten feet. Once south of Pleasonton Avenue it turns due south toward the rocky Trostle meadows where it widens even more, catching runoff from both Cemetery Ridge and a slight rise to the west, the latter stretching toward the Klingle farmyard, 700 yards distant. This rising ground is not a ridge, but an elongated knoll that is part of the Broad Open Plain. Although the flowing run itself is not particularly wide the marshy flood plain extends several dozen yards away from banks that rise from six to eighteen inches above the run.[3]

During the spring rainy season the muddy waters flowing through Plum Run can become torrents two, three, and even four feet deep. During the dryer summer it is not unusual to see one inch of water, sometimes less, stagnating in slowly draining pools. Because it is a catch basin it is almost never completely dry. Even if the run itself is dry the bogs on either side remain moist and soggy. Back-to-back storms in 1989 produced enough water pouring into the run from the Broad Open Plain that a river between four and five feet deep churned southward through the channel, turning the meandering run into a tempest. Mounds of mud were cast against fallen timber and piles of rubbish, creating a nightmare for the National Park Service. Although the run has long since returned to its original course the scars are clearly visible in lower Trostle's Meadows.

Once in the lower meadows the flood plain is dotted with enormous boulders and thousands of large rocks.

Crumbling chunks of shale dot the area as they did back in 1863. Because of the 1989 storms, the terrain west of the run, over which Brig. Gen. William Barksdale's three Mississippi regiments advanced, is somewhat altered. East of the run a small fist-shaped knoll rises ten feet above the run. It too has been altered by years of unchecked growth of foliage and timber. Here too the landscape is littered with rocks and shale. Although the boulders and larger rocks are easy to spot, the crumbling shale and smaller stones are buried beneath a luxuriant carpet of wild and moist sweet grass. Walking can be difficult and even dangerous when one traverses these little-visited lower meadows.

It is not easy to visualize what happened here July Second atop the small fist-shaped knoll[4] east of the run where the 111th New York advanced. The alteration has been so extensive that it is difficult to imagine that anyone could have charged across an open plain and be in turn countered over equally open but higher ground.

The northern reaches of this flood plain, north of the small fist-shaped knoll, and southeast of Codori's meadows near the intersection of the adjoining dry wash, or ravine, have changed little. Although the sprawling Camp Colt covered much of this area it has remained pretty much open over the years. Save for the Low Rough Ground and along the banks of Plum Run, one can still see portions of the Emmitsburg Road as it angles past the Codori farm 800 yards to the west-northwest. Most of the Emmitsburg Road, however, is screened from view to the west by an open rise ascending out of Plum Rum directly west of the fist-shaped knoll. The ground gradually ascends about 20 feet as it extends 200 yards west of the run, then gradually descends into another shallow swale due east of the Klingle house. It is across this open plain and rise that most of Wilcox's Alabamans advanced and descended into Plum Run, supported by Col. David Lang's Florida Brigade following their left-rear in echelon.[5]

At the time of the battle Plum Run's banks varied in undergrowth and brush. Its course through Codori's meadows offered little cover save for a few small trees, scrub oak, and thick brush. As in Trostle's lower meadows numerous boulders and large rocks dotted the landscape east and west of the run, especially along the length referred to today as the Low Rough Ground, where General Hancock was wounded July Third. In 1863 the underbrush was exceptionally thick along the west bank where today's monument dedicated to the 1st Minnesota stands in Plum Run Ravine, about 400 yards west of the Pennsylvania State Monument. All that can be seen from within the ravine is the rising ground of the fist-shaped knoll to the south and the gradually rising hill to the west. Looking west-northwest, however, the entire Broad Open Plain allows a vista beyond the Codori farm to the William Bliss farm west of the Emmitsburg Road.

On July Second there was standing if not slow-running water in Plum Run. The stagnating pools and the limited shade were anything but a respite from the heat. To the contrary, the humidity soared within the Plum Run ravine and mosquitoes were rampant. At 7:00 A.M. on July Second, the position was occupied by regiments from Birney's division. They found little comfort within the low ground they all thought was unfavorable. After Birney departed to relieve Geary's division near Little Round Top the only things remaining near Plum Run below Cemetery Ridge were garbage, rubbish, and bodily waste from thousands of men and a hundred horses.

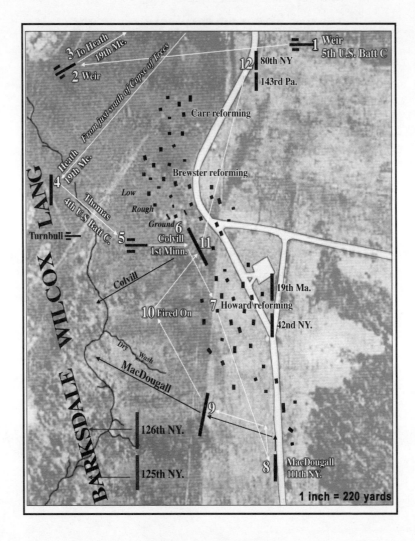

1 Weir
5th U.S. Batt C

12 80th NY

143rd Pa.

Carr reforming

Brewster reforming

3 To Heath
19th Me.

2 Weir

From just south of Copse of Trees

4 Heath
19th Me.

LANG

WILCOX

4th U.S Batt C.

Thomas

Low
Rough
Ground

Turnbull

5

6
Colvill
1st Minn.

11

Colvill

10 Fired On

7 Howard reforming

19th Ma.

42nd NY.

BARKSDALE

Dry Wash

MacDougall

9

126th NY.

125th NY.

8 MacDougall
111th NY.

1 inch = 220 yards

Hancock's Ride

Driving and Walking Tour
Battle Between the Farm Lanes:
Hancock and the Plum Run Ravine
INTRODUCTION

Now that you are familiar with the tactical details of the fight between the Hummelbaugh and Trostle Farm Lanes on July Second, you are ready to take a driving tour to see where the deployments, advance, and action took place. With the exception of the first two stops, most of the field over which Hancock rode is visible at all times. Our tour takes you on a circular route and includes photographs of markers, monuments, and vistas, and an explanation of each stop. Because of the one-way avenues within the park you will have to counter-march only once, along the Emmitsburg Road between the Rogers House and United States (Trostle) Avenue.

Each stop includes a walking tour; some are short, some long. Our purpose is to give you a sense, not only of the battle, but also of the topography and how the features of the landscape exerted a powerful influence on the outcome of this critical portion of the battle. Parts of the field have changed over the years, and where they have, we will describe how it was. We urge you to take time to get a feel for the ground, for its shape and movement. Men marched and charged and fought and died on it, officers deployed their troops based on it, and artillery pieces were placed to take advantage of it. If you pay close attention to it, it will tell you a story.

A simple stroll down the reverse slope of Cemetery

Ridge east of the Copse of Trees will put into perspective the arrival route of Hancock's Second Corps. You will see the actual eminences of that slope, not observable from Hancock Avenue, just a few yards away. The logic of how and why Generals Hays and Gibbon deployed their troops as they did on July Second lies in the ground they covered and how their regiments arrived.

For the longer walks down into and along Plum Run Ravine, keep in mind that there are, at times, cattle roaming about and that it does get hot in the summer. So *take water*. The walk to view the First Minnesota markers in Plum Run is well worth the trek. The view from within the run and ravine where Colvill's Minnesotans made their stand should bring your senses to an emotional high. Not one visitor in a hundred to Gettysburg makes the short walk to this extraordinary spot.

As part of our tour, we include maps and numerous photographs of the players in this violent drama as well as pictures to show approaches, advance routes, and positions within the run and ravine. You will not have to walk far from the stops to understand what occurred.

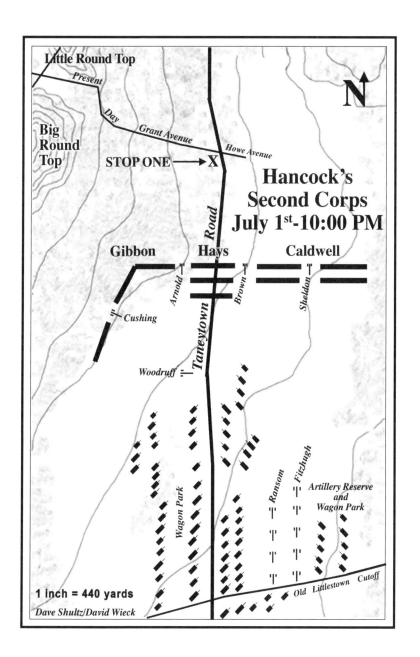

Stop One: July 1st, Evening

Driving and Walking Tour
Stop One:
Howe and Grant Avenues

We start our auto tour east of Little Round Top, where General Hancock's Second Corps filed into the Taneytown Road as dawn broke. The ideal starting point is the intersection of Howe and Grant Avenues (Pa. Rte. 134) at the base of Little Round Top, roughly one-half mile south of present day Wheatfield Road.

Prior to falling in that morning, the Second Corps had stretched in an unbroken crescent-shaped line from

Stop One: Near Center of the Second Corps
Taneytown Road looking north toward Grant/Howe Avenue intersection. Photo depicts the approximate center of Hays's Third Division as it fronted north in the early morning of July Second. Caldwell's First Division was deployed to the right, its right connecting with 16th Pennsylvania Cavalry vedettes 1000 yards to the east.

west to east, its left flank west of the Taneytown Road fronting west-northwest, the right fronting due north, east of the road. Hancock placed his troops in this crescent-shaped position to cover the Union Army in case of retreat. On the march up from Virginia, Caldwell's First Division led the way, followed in turn by the Second and Third Divisions. When they reached this position east of Little Round Top, Caldwell's men turned east, entering the fields near present day Howe Avenue, to cover the right flank. Gibbon's Second Division turned west, covering approaches south of Big Round Top, while Gen. Alexander Hays's Third Division deployed in the center straddling the road. Supported by Hazard's artillery, Hancock's well-developed line was set to cover a Union withdrawal from Cemetery Hill down either the Taneytown Road or Baltimore Pike, while Meade set a new line along the length of Pipe Creek, several miles south. To add strength, General Tyler had two Reserve Artillery Brigades parked less then one-half mile south, near the cutoff road to Littlestown (Hwy 11–15).

Before heading north on the Taneytown Road, take a few moments in Howe Avenue, in order to contemplate Hancock's primary objective, securing the Taneytown Road itself. In order to hold this narrow rural lane, secondary in importance only to the Baltimore Pike, Little Round Top had to be secured—and it was. Between 4:30 and 5:30 A.M., while Hancock's command filed back into the Taneytown Road, the men of Brig. Gen. John W. Geary's First Division, Twelfth Corps, were brewing coffee over small fires on Little

Stop One: Gibbon Anchors the Left
Howe/Grant Avenue intersection looking west-southwest beyond Hays's left flank towards Gibbon's center salient, located above a small run beyond the tree line. Gibbon's extreme left extended far enough to see beyond the spur jutting southward from Big Round Top (seen here on the right of the photograph).

Round Top and along the lower (southern) length of Cemetery Ridge.

One of Geary's attached batteries was posted east of Little Round Top across from the Jacob Weikert farmyard with two infantry regiments supporting it. Fronting east, these units were the first to see Hancock's forward elements approaching on July Second.

It was because of the deployment the night before that Hays's Third Division now led the Second Corps forward. His men had deployed on either side of the road, in the fields south of Howe Avenue, and because they were closest to the road, they now led the way, the First and Second Divisions falling in behind them.

Hancock obviously knew Little Round Top was secured, and with General Sickles's Third Corps slated to relieve that command, his orders were to proceed up the Taneytown Road, bridging the gap between the First Corps's left, near Zeigler's Grove, and Sickles's right, near the Hummelbaugh Farm Lane, or Pleasonton Avenue, as it is now known.

Once on the Taneytown Road, drive north. You will be passing over the same undulating terrain as did the Second Corps. As you drive, take note of the narrow winding valley and its comparative isolation. The rolling fields and open ar-

Stop One: One Crowded Avenue
Taneytown/Granite Schoolhouse Road intersection, looking north, one mile north of Howe Avenue. This road became congested along this entire length within moments after Hancock's troops broke camp at 4:30 A.M.

eas to the west, beyond South Cemetery Ridge, are invisible to you here. You will pass numerous historic buildings beginning with Jacob Weikert's large stone home, west of the road. Markers on buildings indicate structures that were in existence during the battle. Once north of present-day Wheatfield Road, you will ascend a wide-open hill that belonged to Sarah Patterson. She and her older brother, William, whose farm and residence were north of hers, owned tracts of land on either side of the road stretching north for the next mile or so. Looking east, you can see the large Spangler barn, appearing very much as it was during the battle.

Once past the Patterson farm, you will descend into a shallow hollow, then immediately ascend a rise as you near the Granite Schoolhouse Road. Although there were stands of trees here at that time, they were merely wood lots, thinned and maintained, and not the thick woods you see now. You are passing over the ground where the Second Corps was ushered off the road to the right. Passing the William Patterson farm, you will then close on the Schriber, or Fry farm, which stretched north to the Granite Schoolhouse Road.

Once north of the Granite Schoolhouse Road intersection you will be nearing the farm lane in which Capt. Dunbar Ransom, First Regular Artillery Brigade, Artillery Reserve, sat his horse patiently waiting for his batteries to top the sweeping rise belonging to William Patterson. This is our next scheduled stop and is the last stop from which the field of battle cannot be seen. It is, however, every bit as important as the other stops, for the approach of and deployment of Hancock's Second Corps had everything to do with the outcome of the July Second battle to secure the Taneytown Road.

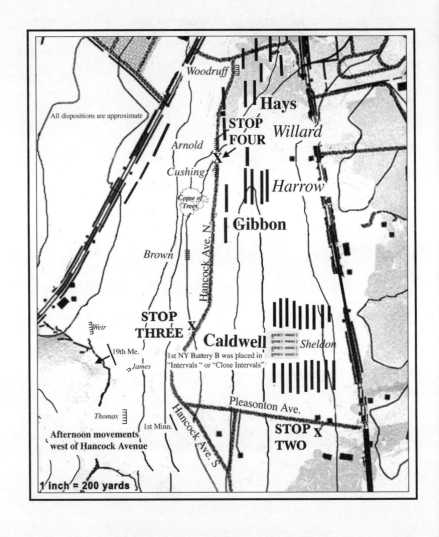

All dispositions are approximate

Woodruff

Hays

STOP
FOUR

Willard

Arnold

Cushing

X

Harrow

Copse of
Trees

Gibbon

Hancock Ave. N

Brown

STOP
THREE   X

Caldwell

Sheldon

Weir

1st NY Battery B was placed in
"Intervals" or "Close Intervals"

19th Me.

James

Pleasonton Ave.

Thomas

1st Minn.

STOP   X
TWO

Hancock Ave. S

**Afternoon movements
west of Hancock Avenue**

1 inch = 200 yards

Stops Two-Four: July 2nd,
Afternoon Movements West of
Hancock Avenue

Driving and Walking Tour
Stop Two:
Taneytown Rd.—Pleasonton Ave.

The intersection of the Taneytown Road and Pleasonton Avenue (Hummelbaugh Farm Lane) is accessible from three directions. Our approach is from the south, the direction from which the Second Corps approached. This route takes you over the same undulating hills and dales that Hancock's men marched in 1863, passing the Patterson farms and woods. Note the countryside as you drive, and be aware that the road you are traveling was approximately twelve feet narrower than it is today.

Stop Two: Hummelbaugh Farm Lane Intersection
Hummelbaugh's farm lane intersection looking north-northwest. Hays and Gibbon's infantry passed over this field as they angled toward the Copse of Trees in the distance.

Stop Two: Hummelbaugh Farm
Taneytown Road north of the intersection looking west-southwest.
Caldwell's initial placement was in this field, his left resting near present-day Pleasonton Avenue, his right near the Peter Frey farm. Note
how irregular the slope is as it gradually rises toward the crest,
some 500 yards distant.

On nearing Pleasonton Avenue, look for the National
Park maintenance building (red brick) on the west side of
the road. Turn left onto Pleasonton Avenue and continue
100 yards to the parking lot on the left (directly across the
road from the Hummelbaugh house & barn). This is STOP
TWO. As you ascend the ridge toward the Hummelbaugh
house and barn note the undulating east slope. As you approach the residence you will be able to see the entire route
taken by the Second Corps as it ascended the ridge, with the
Copse of Trees clearly visible on the crest in the distance.

Once parked and out of the car, take a few moments to look about. Note the open expanse of the eastern, or reverse, slope, of the ridge, and that you cannot see over the crest 400 yards to the west. You can, however, see the Copse of Trees to the north but not the Bryan barn beyond it. Peter Frey's and Lydia Leister's houses are clearly visible, as is Cemetery Hill beyond. Visualize, if you can, Zeigler's Grove beyond the Leister house, and how dominant that stand of trees would have been.

Walk east on Pleasonton Avenue, back toward Taney-town Road, making sure to stop and look at Hummelbaugh house (It is a park service employee residence today, so please do not disturb the residents). This small, white-washed, clap-board house has been restored to its condition during the battle, when it was turned into a field hospital on July Second. Bloody amputated limbs of every description were heaped into fly-ridden piles reaching to the bottom sill of every first-floor window in the home. Col. Edward Warner wrote about the piles of discarded shoes near the barn and the stench of amputated body extremities piled four feet high.

Do not hesitate to explore north, beyond the homestead, where Lt. John G. Turnbull's Third U.S. Batteries F and K Consolidated, were placed in park. Note how, from this an-gle, Cemetery Ridge is wide and open. This was not the case in 1863. At least five orchards dotted the landscape between the Hummelbaugh and Peter Frey farms in 1863 with several more beyond them. Still, note how easy it would be to place three divisions of a single corps by regiments in mass from

Pleasonton Avenue north through Zeigler's Grove (now occupied by the old Visitor Center and parking lot). Here, east of the crest of Cemetery Ridge, those men would be hidden from Confederate eyes.

Captain Ransom was probably nearer the intersection, as the Patterson Woods would have blocked his view south as it does ours today. Because the maintenance shed blocks our view, walk east to the intersection to visualize what the captain experienced. Standing near the monument dedicated to Lt. Edward Heaton's Second U.S., Batteries B and L Consolidated, you will note the Taneytown Road ascending the rise south of the Granite Schoolhouse Road. Although it is impossible to see beyond this rise, the billowing dust kicked up by the approaching Second Corps could easily be seen.

The woods were far less dense in 1863, with plenty of open space dotted with small orchards surrounding both the Patterson and Schriber farms. Major Willard's pioneers were the first to pass over the crest of the rise to your south, passing the intersection and Captain Ransom. Turning to face north, you can see the Peter Frey farmyard in the distance, partially obscured by yet another small rise between that farm and the Hummelbaugh homestead. Beyond what many referred to as Frey's "big stone farm house" lies the Leister residence, the white-washed barn more visible than the small house which General Meade made his headquarters. Again, note the undulating road as it winds north past the Frey and Leister homes, sinking slightly at the Guinn house swale before ascending South Cemetery Hill.

Stop Two: Caldwell, Gibbon, Hays
Taken from atop the Pennsylvania Monument, facing east-northeast.
This photo clearly shows the expansiveness of the eastern slope of
Cemetery Ridge. Caldwell's left front was very near today's Pleasonton/
Humphreys Avenue intersection, seen here in the foreground. The road
slanting off to the right marks the crest of Cemetery Ridge along this
stretch. Caldwell's right was near the Peter Frey farm lane, visible in the
center of the picture, with Gibbon's men beyond the yard. Hays's line
was north of Gibbon, beginning near the Cyclorama,
visible in the distance on the left.

Had you had been standing with Ransom near this
intersection on July Second, 1863, you would have seen and
possibly heard Major Willard issue commands for his pioneers to start dismantling the rail fences bordering both the
Hummelbaugh farm lane and Taneytown Road. As you look
north-northwest, toward the Copse of Trees, you are gazing

over the route taken by Hays's and Gibbon's arriving Third and Second Divisions. Before those columns arrived, however, you would have seen Willard's Hoosiers scale the gentle slope, dismantling at least three rail fences and three pig rails over perpendicular-running stone walls.

To your immediate front is the large open and ascending plain belonging to Hummelbaugh on which General Caldwell first placed his tightly massed First Division. His right flank was very near Gibbon's left, 400 yards distant, one of those stone walls separating the two commands. It is probable that Caldwell's left regiment was near the Hummelbaugh farm lane, possibly south of it. By this time Confederate shot and shell, fired from Seminary Ridge, was plowing up, bounding down, and exploding above the reverse slope you are gazing across. This inaccurate fire was intended to harass and, if possible, damage the arriving Second Corps batteries as they moved along the crest, ascending the ridge using both the Hummelbaugh and Peter Frey farm lanes.

The first Reserve batteries to arrive belonged to Captain Fitzhugh's Third Volunteer Brigade. Following Caldwell, these guns were detoured east, turning right on the Granite Schoolhouse Road. Once Fitzhugh's four batteries were off the Taneytown Road, Ransom's regulars passed over that intersection, heading toward the Hummelbaugh farm lane. Because Caldwell's division deployed in the meadow there was not room enough for all of Captain Ransom's arriving batteries. General Tyler, commanding the Artillery Reserve, and Ransom, had set up their headquarters in the Hummelbaugh barn hoping to secure the fields surrounding that dwelling. Instead, only two of Ransom's batteries were placed there, nearer the Taneytown Road, below Caldwell, with his two other batteries across that avenue to the east. To add to the confusion, the Second Corps's medical staff, anticipating the battle and its casualties, evicted Tyler and Ransom from the barn. Ransom moved his headquarters into a small orchard nearer the Frey farm while Tyler retired to the Schriber barn.

It is not necessary to explore the cut off route, as STOP FOUR will take you to the Copse of Trees. On the next stop we will explore not only the initial deployment of Hays's and Gibbon's divisions, but also some of the Confederate dispositions.

Driving and Walking Tour
Stop Three:
Hancock & Pleasonton Avenues

Once back in the car, continue west past the parking lot and ascend Cemetery Ridge. As you pass the Hummelbaugh residence, note the roughness of the reverse slope south of the farm lane compared to that to the north. Large boulders and rocks once dominated the landscape to the south, as they did Patterson's Woods. Most of the large boulders were removed to make way for a trolley that once ran the length of South Cemetery Ridge, ascending it near the ornate Pennsylvania State Monument.

When you near Hancock Avenue intersection, 200 yards west of the Hummelbaugh farm, you will have reached the crest of Cemetery Ridge. Slow or pull off to the right to look over the flat open crest. Continuing west, you will reach the intersection that was very possibly the most important confluence of two rural roads during the battle on July Second.

When you reach the Hancock–Pleasonton Avenue intersection, bear in mind that in 1863 a rural farm lane paralleled the ridge as Hancock Avenue does today. Looking west you will see how the National Park has attempted to articulate the actual route of the Hummelbaugh–Codori farm lanes as they converged west of and below the crest near the Low Rough Ground. This lane was used as a short cut, or bypass, to the Emmitsburg Road, and was no doubt used by many.

STOP THREE: Wide Open Plain
From a point north of the Low Rough Ground, Wilcox and Lang
advanced over this "Wide Open Plain."

Turn north (right) on Hancock Avenue and stop
near the 16th Vermont monument located on your right. This
marker, although it plays a part in our story, will be the last
monument we visit. What we are here for now are the 19th
Maine's flank markers west of the road, immediately across the
avenue from the 16th Vermont Monument. The flank markers
of the 19th Maine are useful for reference only; that regiment
was initially placed in line of battle 400 yards further north,
nearer the Copse of Trees. The 19th's second position was due
west of these markers, beyond Plum Run, as it bends west
toward its source near the Emmitsburg Road. You are standing in the area in which General Carr reformed his tattered
brigade with Colonel Brewster's men to your immediate left

and front, opposite Codori's rail lined farm lane.

Take a moment and scan the open fields belonging to Nathaniel Codori. The ground over which you are gazing, and over which the 19th Maine countercharged, was altered by Camp Colt. Although it appears relatively untouched, Plum Run itself is not the same body of water that it was in 1863. Although its course is well defined and has not changed, it was once wider and shallower with bogs on both side stretching out for many yards. There were, of course, underbrush, bushes, a few trees, and plenty of cattails. Still, the creek it-

STOP THREE: 19th Maine's Initial Position
The "Wide Open Plain" seen from the 19th Maine's initial position south of the Copse of Trees. Moments before addressing the 19th Maine, Hancock had placed Weir's 5th U.S. Battery C in an exposed position in the area between the bush in the center of the photograph and Codori's barn, seen on the right. Hancock led the 19th Maine past Weir's left, crossing the rural farm lane and traversing the field in the distance, heading toward Plum Run south of the lane.

self at this point was not an impediment to Colonel Heath's men. Also missing are the numerous rocks, commented on by Col. David Lang, commander of Perry's Florida Brigade, which once dotted the landscape about Plum Run. All these rocks and small boulders disappeared when Camp Colt was graded.

Cross back over Hancock Avenue and walk north 100 yards, stopping at the battery marker of the Fifth United States Light Artillery, Battery C, east of the road. Commanded by Lt. Gulian Weir, that battery was first placed near this marker by General Hancock, and is regarded as its first position on July Second. As you look back toward the Codori barn, note Plum Run as it bends toward the west. Weir's second position was about 300 yards east of the barn at an angle to Plum Run and the Emmitsburg Road. Weir's third position was to your front, just beyond the base of the ridge, one hundred or so yards beyond the 80th and 82nd New York Monuments west of the road.

To the right of the 82nd New York marker is a monument to the First Minnesota. This marker represents that regiment's July Third position and not its position on the Second. From where you are standing, or sitting in your vehicle, you are on the ground on which Colonels Gates and Dana reformed their small brigades and over which Col. Francis V. Randall passed with the 13th Vermont. It is near this same ground that General Meade, accompanied by Generals Doubleday and Stannard, led the latter's remaining two regiments onto the crest of Cemetery Ridge.

STOP THREE: Head Waters of Plum Run

Plum Run meanders east-southeast toward Cemetery Ridge from its headwaters south of the Codori barn, north of the Codori/Hummel-baugh crossroad. Weir's 5th U.S. Battery C was first placed near here on July Second. Second Lieutenant Livingston later unlimbered his doomed section near here. The not-so-small tree in the center is the same bush seen in the previous two photographs. The 19th Maine passed, from left to right, east of this spot, double-timing across the farm lane. The rail fence angling away to the left was not an impediment, as Caldwell's pioneers had previously dismantled it.

Before reentering your vehicle, take a moment to look over the field on the reverse slope to the east. Between here and the Taneytown Road is where General Caldwell first placed his division. You are probably in line with and very near his right flank. The division faced west in regiments by brigades, arms stacked, men lying down. The First New York, Battery B, was probably about 100 yards due east of Battery C's marker, with Caldwell's First Division beyond them.

Also note that if Caldwell had placed his division south of Pleasonton Avenue, and the Pennsylvania State Monument, where that division's monument is located, a gap of 1000 yards would have existed between his right and Gibbon's left. At 8:00 that morning, it was still assumed that Sickles was to secure that position. It would have been unorthodox and unsound militarily for Hancock to have split his corps at that time of day.

Driving and Walking Tour
Stop Four:
Copse of Trees—Bryan Farm

Drive north past the Copse of Trees and stop near the Inner Angle. This will place you at the low perpendicular wall that once separated Arnold and Cushing's batteries. It was actually more rubble than wall that connected with today's Inner Angle, running east to the crest where it connected with yet another low wall. It continued down the reverse slope to-

STOP FOUR: Bryan Peach Orchard
Taken from atop the Cyclorama deck. This unique vista shows not only Willard's brigade's initial position in the Bryan Peach Orchard but also their path south to redemption. As they moved south, east of the crest, the "Harpers Ferry Cowards" passed the 106th Pennsylvania (Webb), and then the caisson parks belonging to Arnold and Cushing. The 1st Minnesota and the 19th Maine were initially placed beyond the rail fence in the middle of the picture.

ward the Leister farm, separating General Hays's and General Gibbon's divisions. Willard's Harpers Ferry Cowards lay in reserve on the reverse slope north of the wall, their left flank very near Arnold's right section's caissons, Harrow's brigade laying 100-odd yards south of it, east of Cushing's caissons.

In order to appreciate fully the distinctness of the reverse slope, walk east a little distance down the path leading to the Leister barn, 250 yards away. Walk past the statue of General Meade and note how quickly you descend from the crest. Both Arnold and Cushing had their caissons in this

STOP FOUR: East Slope
Looking east-southeast from opposite the Copse of Trees (beyond the right frame of the picture). Cushing's caisson park would be to the immediate left, along with Harrow's remaining reserves – the 19th Maine and the 1st Minnesota, near remnants of a stone wall marked in this picture by a line of brush. Hays's and Gibbon's divisions traversed the field from right to left as they ascended the slope just north of the Taneytown Road/ Hummelbaugh Farm Lane intersection.

area, just east of the crest with another stone wall separating them from the infantry further east to their rear. As you look both south and north, note how the ground undulates. Imagine what it felt like for the men, lying here just a few feet below the crest, with artillery shells flying and exploding overhead, hearing the noise of combat, and not knowing what was going on just a few yards to the west.

Walk back to Hancock Avenue and cross over it to the Angle. Looking to the west-southwest, beyond the Codori farm, you will see the Henry Spangler farm. To the east-north-east of that residence, and east of the Emmitsburg Road, you will see the Klingle farm. As you scan the Emmitsburg Road back north, toward the Codori farm, you will see the white picket fence that was once the Rogers residence. It was across those fields that Wilcox's Crimson Tide and Lang's Gators passed to reach Plum Run.

This vantage point is very deceiving in that the ground over which you are gazing appears fairly level. It is not. We will explore that a bit later.

Before leaving, walk south to the Copse of Trees. Look toward Plum Run and then Cemetery Ridge, focusing on the Pennsylvania State Monument, noting how both ridge and creek form an inverted salient, or bowl. It was into this bowl that Wilcox's legions advanced. Look west of the run toward the rise located between the Klingle farm and Plum Run. It was onto this rise that the 42nd New York and 19th Massachusetts advanced from near where you are standing. Plum Run Ravine is between that rise and the ridge.

Copse of Trees
Inner Angle
Klingle Farm
Codori Farm

STOP FOUR: West Slope
The "Wide Open Plain" was a slaughter pen from the Copse of Trees
south to Trostle's Lane. Barksdale, Wilcox, and Lang advanced into an
amphitheater of converging Federal forces. Their long, hot, and tiring
march culminated in a bloody struggle within a marshy ravine one-half
miles south of Cushing's battery.

Before leaving STOP FOUR take a few moments
to examine the monuments and markers of each of the regiments who participated in the fight between the farm lanes.

Return to your car and continue north. As you drive
you will pass the Bryan farm and Zeigler's Grove. Remember as you leave Cemetery Ridge that all the while they were
there, the men on the crest and reverse slope were under Confederate artillery fire as the infantry along Emmitsburg Road
engaged with Confederates in the William Bliss farm, 800
yards west of the Bryan barn.

At the next intersection turn left, then left again onto the Emmitsburg Road. Once on the Emmitsburg Road please do not stop. Drive approximately 1.1 miles to present day United States Avenue. As you travel southwest over the Emmitsburg Road you are passing the positions defended by General Carr's brigade and Lt. John G. Turnbull's 3rd United States Light Artillery, Batteries F and K Consolidated, and Lt. Francis Seeley's 4th United States Light Artillery, Battery K. It was over this same ground and road that Wilcox advanced, crushing Carr's left and Seeley's battery near the Klingle house. You are also passing where Colonel Lang pressed back Carr's right and Turnbull's battery near the Rogers house, west of the road.

Turn left on United States Avenue, travel an additional 100 yards to Sickles Avenue, then turn left again. You are now facing north. Because it is dangerous to park along the Emmitsburg Road, STOP FIVE is here, on Sickles Avenue.

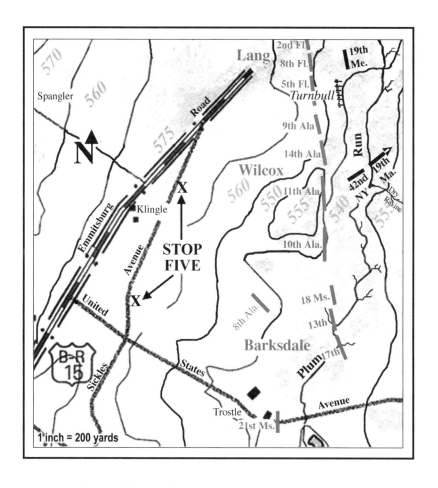

Stop Five: Later in the afternoon.
The Confederates Advance Across the
Emmitsburg Road

Driving and Walking Tour
Stop Five:
Sickles & United States Avenues

STOP FIVE is unique in that you can see virtually the entire field over which Barksdale, Wilcox, and Lang advanced, and over which Hancock's and Sickles's combined corps resisted. Sickles Avenue, north of United States Avenue, is one of the least visited boulevards within the National Park, at least west of Cemetery Ridge.

Once on Sickles Avenue your counter march will begin. Continue north about 300 yards to the plaque dedicated to Wilcox's Alabama Brigade and stop. For the hardier souls, we suggest that a walk back to Emmitsburg Road and Seeley's 4th U.S. Battery K marker and guns, south of the Klingle farmyard is well worth the effort (Be aware that it is dangerous to pull over by that monument even though there is a turn out). As you walk south to United States Avenue you are facing the ground over which Barksdale's left flank and Wilcox's right advanced on an oblique to that avenue, heading in a north-northeasterly direction.

The Trostle barn is to your left and front as you head south. To your immediate left is the famous Trostle Meadow, descending into Plum Run Ravine, not 400 yards away. On your walk back to Emmitsburg Road, note that you cannot see over the crest of the rise until you are almost on the road itself. Once near the Emmitsburg Road stop at the intersection. Note the undulating fields west of it. It was over these fields that Wilcox advanced, the 8th Alabama bringing up the rear

STOP FIVE: Trostle's Meadow
Sickles/United States Avenue (Trostle's Lane) intersection looking due east. At the time of the battle, Trostle's Lane was much narrower than today's United States Avenue and in fact ran several yards north of the present day road. East of Plum Run, Trostle's Lane curved to the east-northeast, toward the marker and cannons representing Watson's 5th U.S. Battery I. The field and ravine in the foreground was hotly contested, with Barksdale's Mississippians moving across it, and into it, from right to left.

in reserve.

It was the 8th Alabama that last crossed the Emmitsburg Road—Trostle Lane intersection. Moving on an oblique line, it followed Wilcox's principal line as it moved east–northeast. If you face about and gaze across the descending fields in that direction, looking toward the dome of the Pennsylvania State Monument, you will be in line with their advance, which by the way was heading directly toward Colonel Colvill's First Minnesota. The 8th crossed over the intersection moving across an already bloody field, angling into a gap between Barksdale's left regiment, the 18th Mississippi, and Wilcox's right, the 10th Alabama, as those two regiments moved away from each other, the 21st Mississippi detaching itself to advance due east, down the lane that is today's Trostle's Avenue.

For those who wish to walk to Seeley's monument, bear in mind that his battery sat at slight right angles to the road where their marker is placed, the left gun east of the road, the right gun in it. With the plank fence to their front dismantled, their initial target was Barksdale's line along Millerstown Road before they turned their attention to the Confederate batteries unlimbering near the Staub house and Spangler Woods. They then focused on Wilcox's line as it emerged from Henry Spangler's wood lot. Hit by Confederate batteries firing from the McMillian Woods and from Millerstown Road, Battery K was enfiladed from both flanks as well as its front.

There was simply too much pressure on Seeley for his cannoneers to concentrate solely on Wilcox. The effectiveness was further inhibited when Federal infantry west of Emmitsburg Road masked their field of fire even as Wilcox was closing in. Note that, from where you are standing at Battery K's monument, you cannot see into the first swale west of the road. Now imagine hundreds of Union infantry pouring back onto the Emmitsburg Road Rise from that direction and from the south, followed by Barksdale. Wilcox and his men disappear into that swale. Lieutenant Seeley, already wounded, simply ordered double canister and told his men to wait.

Look north, toward the Klingle house and beyond.

Again, you cannot see into the swale west of the road, and more importantly, beyond the Roger's house, west of Emmitsburg Road. By this time Lang's Floridians were closing, pressing back General Carr's blue-clad Yankees at an alarming rate, having flanked them out of their position beyond the white picket fence in the distance. Lang's marker can be viewed when we continue north on our countermarch. Walk back to Sickles Avenue, then take a moment and scan Trostle's Meadows and the monument to the 9th Massachusetts Battery in the

STOP FIVE: Wilcox's Advance

Wilcox's Monument., representing his Alabama brigade. Note how different this terrain is from that over which Barksdale advanced. Here it is more open as it gradually descends toward Plum Run. The low knoll south of Thomas, west of Plum Run, which was defended by the 19th Maine and the 42nd New York, is visible beyond the marker. Though it appears small from this western vantage, it is quite precipitous within the ravine itself. Control of this ravine was paramount. This field was also hotly contested by Humphreys's veterans, who grudgingly gave way as they retired toward Cemetery Ridge in the distance.

distance. Again, note how quickly the rise you are on descends once you are east of the Emmitsburg Road.

Drive north 200 yards, then stop at the marker dedicated to Humphreys's First Division. The Klingle House and barn should be to your immediate left, west of the avenue. You are standing on ground initially defended by the 12th New Hampshire and 16th Massachusetts Infantry, supported by Turnbull's Consolidated Batteries F and K. Note the 26th Pennsylvania Monument, 100 feet to the north, east of the road. It was this regiment that counter-charged, buying Turnbull time to get his guns away as he withdrew at fixed prolonge.

Assailed by Wilcox's left wing, and portions of Lang's right regiment, the 5th Florida, Turnbull retired east toward Plum Run. As you face east, note the small seemingly unimpressive rise, or knoll, separating the Emmitsburg Road Rise from that of Plum Run. It was on the reverse slope of this rise that the 19th Massachusetts and 42nd New York lay, west of and above Plum Run. The walk to Turnbull's Marker crosses the ground where his caissons were probably parked, if they were not further down the slope.

As you look west, across the road, the ground can tell you a story. You can see why Turnbull's battery must have been west of the avenue. It is impossible to see over the crest of the Emmitsburg Road Rise when you are in the road or east of it. It is evident that Turnbull's battery was due south of the picket fence you are fronting, on the crest above the swale in which Captain Ransom made his daring ride to reconnoiter a front already swarming with Confederate infantry. To have an effective field of fire, Turnbull's battery must have been farther west, beyond the crest of that rise.

Before walking back to your car, take time to scan the meadows east of the road, from the Codori farmyard to the Copse of Trees, then south to the Pennsylvania State Monument. You can clearly see the marker and guns of Weir's 5th Battery C, which we viewed at STOP THREE.

Take time to look carefully over the field you inspected from Cemetery Ridge. See how different it is in appearance and how a simple change of direction changes everything. If you get the feeling you are higher than Cemetery Ridge, you are correct. You are actually almost 12 feet higher here than where Pleasonton Avenue intersects Hancock Avenue. The lowest point of the Emmitsburg Road Rise, south of Codori's barn, is four feet higher than the highest point of Cemetery Ridge between Zeigler's Grove and the Wheatfield Road.

Get back into your car, drive to the intersection with the Emmitsburg Road, and turn south (left). Now that you have taken time to inspect the Emmitsburg Road Rise and Klingle farm line, does it look different, more interesting and inviting, this time around, than if you simply winged past it to get to the Wheatfield Road? Head back to United States Avenue and turn east as before. Do not turn left onto Sickles Avenue this time, but continue east, toward the Trostle house. Be aware that today's lane is not the rural lane that existed in 1863. At that time, this small lane passed much closer to the house, within a few feet of it, descending toward Plum Run a good 20 feet north of where it does today.

If you pull over near the farmyard there is access north of the road that leads into the meadows beyond the barn. For anyone who loves to get an intimate view of this battlefield this is one great walk. No trail is needed. Just walk through the opening in the fence and continue north-northeast past the monument to Sickles's wounding. Stop for a moment and look west. You cannot see Sickles Avenue from this position, let alone the Emmitsburg Road. As you continue on, you are descending into South Plum Run Ravine. Barksdale's Mississippians traversed these same bloody fields, heading toward disaster. Willard's "Harpers Ferry Cowards," as well as several of McGilvery's guns, pounded Barksdale's men in this hollow as his men attempted to gain the creek and the rise east of it. Instead, they were caught in a swampy morass with advancing infantry closing from above, and canister and shrapnel devastating them from perfect right enfilade.

Continue north, following Barksdale's line as it wheeled east, in echelon. You will come to the knoll over which the 111th New York counter-charged. Due north of you is the reverse slope west of the creek that housed the 42nd New York and 19th Massachusetts. It was over this ground that Wilcox's right wing took possession of Plum Run. Beyond the rise west of the creek is where Turnbull's battery ended up.

On the walk back to your car, make sure to take time to explore the Trostle farm and pay your respects to the 9th Massachusetts Battery. Once on the move and east of Plum Run, you will immediately begin ascending Cemetery Ridge. To your left on the lower brow of the ridge stand a brace, or section, of cannons, and two monuments. These markers are dedicated to Watson's 5th U.S. Battery I, and the 39th New York. You have just traveled the route of the 21st Mississippi as that regiment carried the 9th Massachusetts and Watson's batteries.

Even if you choose not to walk to those monuments, you should bear in mind that Watson's guns were actually south of Trostle's farm lane, not north, and that today's United States Avenue is at this point a good 40 yards south of the original farm lane. Still, the walk to those monuments is worth the effort. The view from those monuments is spectacular. You can see the length of Plum Run as it winds from north to south. You can see the Peach Orchard and South Cemetery Ridge as well as Warfield and South Seminary Ridges. More importantly for our purposes, you can see the ground over which the Garibaldi Guards charged, from the direction of the State of New York Monument, 350 yards away, driving back the 21st Mississippi and recapturing Watson's battery. You can also see how Lockwood's reinforcements from the Twelfth Corps arrived, advancing across Plum Run to Trostle's farmyard, recapturing Capt. Bigelow's battery in the process.

The object of STOP FIVE has been to introduce you to the terrain of Plum Run Ravine and Cemetery Ridge. Even in the middle of this seemingly open battlefield there are swales and ravines where entire regiments could disappear, or become isolated, and lose touch with other units.

Get back in your car and continue east to the George Weikert farmyard. As you reach this intersection, be aware that this intersection was in existence in 1863, with the lane you are on continuing through Patterson's Woods to the Taneytown Road.

Turn left on Hancock Avenue. Travel 200 yards to the New York State Monument. STOP SIX will be the first of two stops on this part of the ridge that lies between the Trostle and Hummelbaugh Farm Lane.

STOP FIVE: Watson's Battery

The view from Watson's U.S. Battery I, facing west-southwest. The position of the marker is deceptive and incorrect. At the time of the battle, Trostle's rural lane was not the road it is today (United States Avenue) either in width or location. Watson actually unlimbered south of the lane. His field of fire was more to the left of the barn (left-center of photograph) on George Weikert's farm. The 21st Mississippi passed around the barn while crossing the avenue. The 39th New York's right flank was near this position with Watson's four Parrotts nearer the lane to the left. Barksdale passed from left to right.

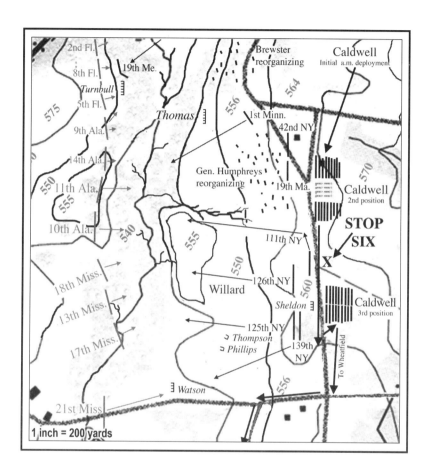

Stop Six: Overview of Federal Positions; Caldwell's Division Has Gone to Help Sickles; the Confederates Advance; Hancock Counters.

Driving and Walking Tour
Stop Six:
Hancock Avenue: Cemetery Ridge

You have just stopped where General Caldwell placed his First Division after having been halted, the first time that his division was sent to aid the Third Corps. After you turned north on Hancock Avenue, you passed the statue of Father William Corby, Irish Brigade Chaplin, who gave absolution to the men of that brigade before they headed south the third and last time. Corby's statue is just to the south, on the east side of Hancock Avenue. Hancock was present when Caldwell's division finally moved off the ridge, leaving Lt. Albert Sheldon's First New York, Battery B, on the crest near the New York State Monument.

When the general returned north from the area of STOP SIX he made a mental note of Battery B. His exact route is not known as he returned toward STOP THREE, passing Colonel Colvill's Minnesotans west-northwest of the Pennsylvania State Monument. It was after his return from this trip that things began to heat up. About this time, Lieutenant Turnbull's Consolidated Batteries F and K came thundering over the crest near him. We will review that shortly.

Step out of your car and take a few moments to scan the ridge. The monuments and markers along this avenue are for useful for reference only and may not indicate the exact positions of the particular units. As you look south from where you are standing, imagine it as it was, with Little Round Top,

Houck's Ridge, the Wheatfield, Stony Hill, Trostle's Woods, and the Peach Orchard, all encased in battle smoke.

Closer to where you are, reserve batteries were rumbling through the intersection you just passed. After Caldwell had left for the Wheatfield, only Battery B stood on the crest between near where you are and the First Minnesota's right flank, approximately 200 yards north. Third Corps fugitives were already regrouping near Sheldon's New Yorkers, with many more retiring from the direction of Plum Run and Trostle's Avenue.

Walk west of Hancock Avenue a few yards. You are now where Colonel Willard reformed his New York regiments, from left to right, the 39th, 125th, and 126th, with the 111th in reserve to their rear. As you face west again, to your immediate front is the open flat knoll that descends into Plum Run and Trostle's Meadow beyond. Turning about 45 degrees to your left, you will see the monument to Watson's battery that you just visited, 100 yards distant. You are looking over the ground traversed by the 139th New York as that regiment moved by the left flank on the double quick, continuing perhaps 150 yards nearer Trostle's Avenue. After facing back, the Garibaldi Guards charged west-southwest in the direction of the marker north of and above United States Avenue.

For those who choose to walk the terrain over which the 125th and 126th charged, you need not cross the rail fence to your front, as we will explore the ravine from the next stop. The fence itself, however, is worth visiting. It is at this fence that Captains Phillips, Thompson, and Dow placed their guns to sweep Plum Ravine and Trostle's Meadows, mauling Barksdale's exposed right wing as it angled past. The line of guns where you are now standing is referred to as McGilvery's line, and these guns not only played a major part in the repulse on July Second but, with Lieutenant James's section,

STOP SIX: Willard's Field

Looking south-southeast across the field toward the New York Monument (seen in the distance at the tree line), where they had been left in reserve by Colonel Willard. General Hancock led the MacDougall and the 111th New York north, then west, ordering them in from just south of a small dry wash that descended and emptied into Plum Run. Charging from left to right, the 111th was already taking casualties by the time it reached this position. To the immediate south of MacDougall, Willard's three remaining regiments, the 125th, 126th, and 39th New York, were already earning bloody redemption for Harpers Ferry.

Even from a short distance, the terrain appears relatively flat. It is anything but and it was worse at the time of the battle. Rocks and shale were scattered about a field too rugged for cultivation.

4th U.S., Battery K, placed north of Trostle's Avenue, near present day United States Avenue, anchored the left of this line on July Third.

If you choose to walk the field west of the New York State Monument, start out by angling west-northwest. In doing so, you will travel the route of the 126th New York. Looking to your right, you will see the ground over which Colonel MacDougall's 111th charged, his left 150 yards away, as his regiment angled slightly to the north, opening a gap between it and the 126th that would present an opportunity to the advancing Confederates. From the rail fence you can see the depression in which some of Wilcox's Alabamans, and Barksdale's Mississippians, actually penetrated the gap between the 111th's left and 126th's right, the latter a few yards in advance.

As you walk back towards the New York Monument, please note that by the time Willard's men charged, Battery B had disappeared to the south, nearer the George Weikert farm. Since Hancock did not know that Willard's brigade was on the ridge he was very probably looking for Battery B when, after conversing with Humphreys, he happened on the 111th New York. It was in this field and in Patterson Woods beyond the New York Monument where 12th Corps reinforcements solidified this part of the line before being recalled to the Baltimore Pike later in the evening.

Before stepping onto the asphalt of Hancock Avenue look northwest, toward the Codori farm, 250 yards distant. You should be able to see part of what is left of the dry ravine, together with the knoll over which the 111th New York charged. That knoll blocks your view of the descending field over which the First Minnesota charged and where Thomas's 4th New York, Battery C was placed. The trees indicating the location of the Low Rough Ground, where Brewster re-formed, are visible, as is the Codori farm beyond. The rising knoll west of Thomas's battery's position is not visible but will be from our next stop.

Return to your car and drive slowly north. You are nearing Humphreys Avenue. Hancock approached the 111th New York from the opposite direction after having spoken with General Humphreys near the intersection now bearing the names of the two generals. Once you cross that intersec-tion the dry ravine will be to your left, angling west-northwest, as it descends toward Plum Run. Hancock was returning to-ward Thomas's battery north of the ravine when he was fired

STOP SIX: The 111th New York's Redemption
Seen from atop the Pennsylvania Monument, facing southeast. The
111th New York charged across this field on an oblique from left to right.
MacDougall's Knoll can be seem at the right-center of the photograph,
near the edge of the picture.

on from the direction of Plum Run. To his rear, Humphreys was still reforming near where you have just passed, while the 111th was charging over the knoll south of the ravine.

As you near the Pennsylvania State Monument, and more importantly for our purposes, the First Minnesota Monument, note the field to your left. This is the open field south of Thomas on which Humphreys's reformed line returned fire and over which Colonel Colvill's Minnesotans charged. Hancock was probably fired on very near the rail fence in the distance, the same rail fence you just visited. Also note Caldwell's First Division marker east of the avenue. This marker is the approximate position of that division's position when it was first sent south, before being recalled to the area of STOP SIX.

Pull to the right and stop at the Pennsylvania State Monument. You are at STOP SEVEN, the last of the stops relating to our study within this area of the field. Two additional stops, offering a different perspective, will be described after we leave STOP SEVEN.

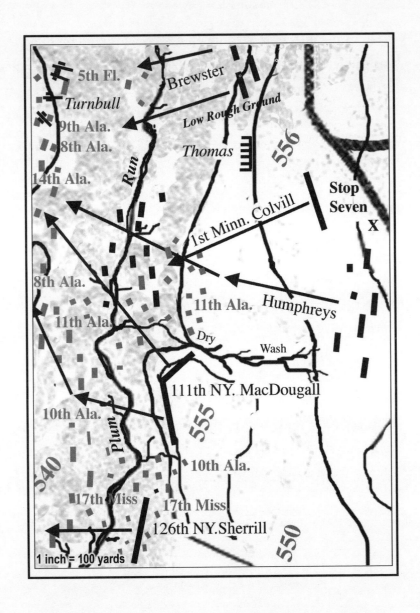

Stop Seven: Collision in Plum Run Ravine

Driving and Walking Tour
Stop Seven:
Hancock Avenue: Plum Run Ravine

You have traveled a quarter of a mile after leaving STOP SIX. It is worth recalling at this point that Caldwell's First Division was sent south of Hummelbaugh's farm lane around noon, shortly before the First Minnesota was sent to Thomas's support. When Caldwell took up his second position, his right flank was well south of the Pennsylvania State Monument with his center beyond the Humphreys-Hancock

STOP SEVEN: Thomas's Battery C
Thomas's Battery's right flank was very near here, the Low Rough Ground to his right and rear, his caisson park on the gentle slope east of his gun line. The northern part of the low knoll west of the run that hampered the 1st Minnesota's advance can bee seen beyond the trees. That was where Lieutenant Turnbull's 3rd U.S. Battery fought hand-to-hand. During that fight the 19th Maine's left company was refused to form a salient facing south just beyond the tree line.

Avenues intersection, nearer to the Second Division's plaque.

Had Caldwell's Division been closer to Thomas rather than south of the Pennsylvania State Monument, no doubt Caldwell, and not Gibbon, would have been called upon to furnish troops to that sector of the battlefield. Another indication that Caldwell's Division was to be sent south is that no skirmishers were sent west from this, his second position. He would not have done this if, indeed, his division had been slated to secure that position on the ridge at that time. His skirmishers would in all probability have been as far west as the Klingle house, having passed through General Humphreys's bivouac in Trostle's Meadow and along Plum Run. Further, his skirmishers would have secured the rise located immediately west of Plum Run. They did neither.

As it stands, Caldwell assumed his second position with undefined orders, having been instructed to wait. Hancock still anticipated that Sickles would pull General Humphreys's division back. It was not until that division was seen moving south that Hancock realized Sickles was not going to adhere to the general plan. Shortly thereafter, Longstreet opened the ball and, as Meade had suggested to Sickles, the enemy would not allow him to realign the Third Corps to conform to general orders.

Before starting on your walk you may want to scan the field from the commanding vantage point atop the Pennsylvania State Monument. From the deck high above, you can see the ground over which not only the First Minnesota and 111th New York charged, but also where all the reinforcements

STOP SEVEN: Brewster's Low Rough Ground

Seen from the Low Rough Ground facing due west, where the 19th Maine faced about for the last time and counter-charged. Brewster successfully massed enough troops to fill the gap between the 19th Maine's left flank and Thomas's right section. Anging slightly to the left of the frame, Brewster led his ragtag line toward the low knoll, recapturing a portion of Turnbull's overrun battery. The 19th Maine, on the other hand, slowly moved forward south of the lane in a steady line toward Plum Run, pressing Lang's Floridians before them. Their advance is marked by the rail fence to the left-center of the photograph. Shortly thereafter, Union reinforcements charged through the Codori fields north of the lane, securing the position. Lieutenant Livingston's two captured Napoleons were to the front, on the Emmitsburg Road, having been hauled back by men of the 2nd Florida. On the evening of July 2nd, they were mistaken for Confederate guns.

converged, coming from north, south, and east of those two regiments. You can see the Low Rough Ground to the west-southwest and the rise west of Plum Run. More importantly, you can see how Cemetery Ridge falls away just beyond the rail fence.

It was near that rail fence, 200 yards distant, in a direct line with the Codori farmyard, that young Lieutenant Thomas placed his five Napoleons, the Low Rough Ground to his immediate right. The First Minnesota lay due west of the Pennsylvania State Monument, Colvill's right flank near the marker and guns dedicated to Thomas's 4th U.S. Battery C, his left close to the marker and guns dedicated to the July Third position of Pennsylvania Independent Batteries C and F Consolidated, both west of Hancock Avenue. The First

STOP SEVEN: First position of the 1st Minnesota
Looking south from the Hancock/Pleasonton Avenue intersection, slightly north of the Pennsylvania Monument. Here is where Colonel Colvill's 1st Minnesota dressed ranks before their charge. They were supporting Thomas's 4th U.S. Battery C, which was in position 300 yards west of ther egiment, covering Plum Run Ravine, noted in the distance. During their charge, Colvill led his men over the open field, passing to the left of Thomas.

Minnesota's left flank was a good 100 yards north of their ornate monument located west of the present day Hancock-Humphreys Avenue intersection, where General Humphreys was reforming his small band.

Before leaving the platform, look southeast to the fence-lined avenue we discussed and visited at STOP TWO, leading out to the Codori farm and Emmitsburg Road just north of the Low Rough Ground. By the time Colonel Heath's 19th Maine double-timed through, Caldwell's pioneers had dismantled much of that rail fence. It is near that fence, west of Pleasonton Avenue, where we will begin our walking tour of Plum Run Ravine.

For a comfortable walk we suggest that you wear high walking boots or tube socks with your trousers tucked into them. These informal leggings will ward off ticks and other insects. Make sure that you carry a container of water when you enter the field through the opening in the rail fence running north/south just north of the 17th Maine marker. Watch your step as you walk, for the ground is rocky and uneven. As you enter this small opening, you are passing over the ground where the left flank of General Carr's broken regiment was reforming to the rear of Brewster. The latter was to your front and right and Turnbull's captured battery was due west, west of Plum Run.

The 19th Maine was battling alongside Turnbull's cannoneers to your right and front as you walk west, beyond the marker dedicated to Hancock's Wounding on July Third. As you continue toward Plum Run you are approaching Turnbull's last position, where he and his men fought the Confederates hand to hand. Upon reaching Plum Run look toward the Codori barn and you will be gazing over the ground Lieutenant Livingston's right section traversed as it dashed to break out, only to be captured north of the run where it bends west. Lieutenant Weir's six Napoleons were to your immediate right, 300+ yards distant, beyond the rail-lined farm lane, where they battled to save themselves, as Lang's Floridians and Wright's Georgians engulfed them from their right and rear as they fronted south-southwest. Lieutenant James's two Napoleons were to Colonel Brewster's immediate right, just beyond the Low Rough Ground, north of the rail fence.

When you reach Plum Run note that there are no rocks and boulders beyond the Low Rough Ground, contrary to what Colonel Lang described. The entire area west of the creek was graded when Camp Colt was constructed in the early twentieth century. Due west of where you are standing, there was once an immense parade ground surrounded by several buildings and hundreds of tents, not to mention kitchens, latrines, temporary field warehouses, and officer's quarters. Because of the reshaping of this area in 1917, it is all but impossible to mark exact locations of engaging regiments and batteries.

Crossing Plum Run here places you near Turnbull's right flank, the Rogers picket fence visible west of the Emmitsburg Road. The rise west of Plum Run is due south of you and the Klingle barn is 800 yards west of that. The 19th Massachusetts and 42nd New York lay near the crest of that rise awaiting developments. To appreciate fully the significance and strategic importance of this rise, you should scale its heights. As you mount it you will see that it blocks the view toward Cemetery Hill of all those approaching from the south and from east of the road.

Take a few moments on the crest of the rise to scan 360 degrees. The swale between you and the Klingle house is the same swale that masked Kemper's Virginia Brigade on July Third, as that line headed north-northeast. Not until that body of men moved north of this rise would it be it exposed to Col. Freeman McGilvery's line of artillery placed along the rail fence east of and above Plum Run.

Barksdale was approaching from due south of you on July Second, while Wilcox came from the direction of the Klingle farm. Wilcox's center was directed toward you, having approached in echelon from the direction of the Emmitsburg Road Rise, our STOP FIVE. His right crossed the road first, south of the Klingle house, his far left approaching from north of Klingle's barn, the 8th Alabama bringing up the rear.

Looking north you will see a wide, open plain. Over that undulating plain Lang's Floridians and Wright's Georgians caught hell from every conceivable direction, but pressed on, their lines thinning with every foot of ground gained. Note the Emmitsburg Road Rise as that avenue bends almost east between the Rogers house and the Codori farm. Because General Carr's right was basically in the air west of that rise, his line was easily flanked and enfiladed. As Carr's line collapsed from left to right, Turnbull was also flanked because

STOP SEVEN: MacDougall's Knoll from Plum Run
Looking due east from Plum Run toward the rising ledge where the
11th New York appeared with shocking suddenness. Their double rank
seemed to rise out of the ground,, firing down into the ravine and the
stunned men of the 10th and 11th Alabama regiments. The photograph is
deceptive in that the slope of the knoll is very precipitous – rising about
12 feet at a sharp angle. A man trying to climb it would have to scramble
on all fours. This was the right-center of MacDougall's line, which extended about 200 yards around the bend from the 1st Minnesota's left.

his guns were engaging to the west-southwest. The Rogers
homestead now screened Lang's Floridians as they pressed
forward, forcing Turnbull's guns back from right to left.

From your position east of the road, you can easily
see the distance Turnbull's 3rd U.S had to cover while retiring. With Wilcox's Alabamans pressing his left and front, and
Lang's line almost behind him, Turnbull's slow and methodical withdrawal was accomplished at fixed prolonge, with the
enemy just yards away. Carr's infantry was also withdrawing,

not in a disorganized rout, but rather facing back time and again, as the line slowly made its way east.

Walking back whence you came, re-cross Plum Run where Turnbull's battery was overrun. Once east of the run, ascend the ridge toward the rail fence. You are now at the position occupied by Lieutenant Thomas's Battery C. Looking in the direction of the Pennsylvania State Monument, you can see where the First Minnesota lay, unseen by Thomas. South of where you are standing is the open field off that battery's left flank, with the dry ravine beyond. Beyond the ravine is

STOP SEVEN: Plum Run Ravine
Looking due east from within the Plum Run Ravine. The 1st Minnesota charge originated from left of the frame, north of the Pennsylvania Monument. In the lower left foreground are the remnants of the dry wash. MacDougall's right flank came over the rise on the right. Colvill's battered left flank was anchored in this hollow with the rest of the regiment winding northward in the ravine toward Thomas's Battery C.

the knoll over which the 111th New York charged.

You have already visited the open knoll where Colonel MacDougall led his New Yorkers, and where the First Minnesota lay on the crest. We shall traverse the open field toward the dry ravine, slowly descending toward Plum Run as we angle south-southwest. Look to your left as you walk and note the ridge as it crests. You are entering a sort of hollow with MacDougall's knoll looming above you as you descend. You are crossing the same hallowed field over which Colvill's First Minnesota charged. Note the rise you just visited west of the run and how the run itself curves back toward the Low Rough Ground before sweeping due north and then west toward Emmitsburg Road.

Here, in Plum Run is where the Confederate thrust was blunted. First here were Colvill and his men. In this hollow, you can sense their isolation. When they began their charge, they were almost alone on the field. To the east, the field Colvill's men had just crossed is covered with the dead and dying. North, there is nothing but thick smoke and sheets of flame erupting from battle lines on raised ground, not 20 yards away. Also there is Thomas, his cannons belching fire, delivering loads of canister, many of those canister rounds striking the very ravine where you are standing. The Rebels appear to have overrun the position, but they have not. They are on the rise west of Plum Run as that creek bends away to the northeast, firing point blank at the Minnesotans at right enfilade.

The right and center of Colvill's line is being ham-

STOP SEVEN: Knoll West of and above Plum Run

The 1st Minnesota's line was spread across Plum Run, seen beyond the eastern bank in the foreground, its irregular front stretching beyond both frames of the photograph. Pressed back across the low ground, the men of the 11th Alabama regained some composure as they faced back from atop the knoll pictured west of and above the low ground. The 8th Alabama moved up to support them, creating a living hell for Colvill's Minnesotans. The colonel was wounded in the center of the tree line. The trees seen here were not present at the time of the battle, but the brush was higher than a horse.

mered as he goes down, hit several times, but still he controls his thinning line. From the rise to his immediate front the enemy is trying to counter as his men hold their contested creek bed, firing from what cover they have, bodies in both blue and gray lying in crumpled heaps. On the left, the men have slight cover as the western bank is slightly higher and the brush thicker.

The First Minnesota is down to a fraction of its original force when the enemy above its left wing begins to waver. The 111th New York has just struck Wilcox's right wing and his men pour volley after volley into the shocked Confederates. Even the arrival of the 8th Alabama does not help Wilcox. When that regiment's irregular line crowds into the rear of his wavering line it only creates more chaos. Grudgingly the Alabama line begins to pull back up and over the rise.

And then, the 111th New York comes barreling off the knoll above Colvill's exposed left flank, wheeling almost due north, rolling up Wilcox's skedaddling line from right to left. Into Plum Run they pour, charging up and over the western bank, angling toward the rise west of remnants of the First Minnesota. Colvill blacks out from shock and loss of blood, never realizing that Colonel MacDougall's "Harpers Ferry Cowards" have not only cleared his immediate front, but that they have charged over the rise and recaptured Turnbull's left section as that brace of guns sat where they were taken, then wrecked and dismantled by Thomas's relentless canister fire.

From the east, another line passes through the First Minnesota's left and center where Colonel Colvill lies unconscious. This is the counter-charge of General Humphreys's irregulars, pressing back Wilcox's last line of resistance. Thereafter several more lines of reinforcements pass through the First Minnesota's decimated ranks in Plum Run Ravine. The firing around this bloodied regiment slackens. Lieutenant Thomas's smoothbores cease firing to the right and rear. The Union line and the Taneytown Road are saved as blue-clad legions retake the rise west of the First Minnesota. This important rise will be handed over to Colonel Berdan and his Sharpshooters with plenty of support stretching from near the Rogers farm south to Trostle's Lane.

The charge of the First Minnesota stopped Wilcox's advance, but this success would only have been momentary had not the 111th New York caved in the Alabama flank and proceeded to roll it up. Colonel MacDougall's volunteers saved the First Minnesota from annihilation. The 111th's charge, combined with Humphreys's support and Thomas's fire off the flanks, broke the forces opposing Colvill's men in the run.

After experiencing Plum Run where the 111th New York and First Minnesota helped repulse Wilcox's legions, you will want to scour the ravine below the knoll from which the 111th counter charged. For those who did not experience this portion of the field from STOP FIVE or SIX, Trostle's Avenue, a short walk south, will be rewarding as you visit where Willard's remaining regiments clashed with General Barksdale's Mississippians.

The return to Cemetery Ridge is simple; just walk from the First Minnesota's markers within the run back toward Pleasonton Avenue. As you retrace the steps of that regiment's charge and ascend the crest, look about you again. With your added perspective, note how the shape, the swell and hollow of the ground, dictated the lines of advance of the various units and the positions of the guns.

Once back on Hancock Avenue take a few moments to rest and reflect on what you have seen. The area you have just left, as desperately contested as any in the battle, is too rarely visited. Consider too, how many units converged on that small area of ground.

While many officers and men deserve great credit for the stopping the Confederate advance—Colvill and MacDougall, Thomas and Turnbull and Weir, Brewster and Humphreys and many others—above all it was General Hancock who was responsible for stopping Wilcox when the way to the Union rear lay open. It was the general who personally sent in the 12 units, including the First Minnesota and 111th New York, that hit Wilcox and stopped his brigades from penetrating along Plum Run Ravine.

We have included two additional stops which, while not strictly part of our narrative, offer some additional insights into the drama of the day. To view these stops, drive to West Confederate Avenue, STOP EIGHT, to see the field from an entirely different perspective.

Driving and Walking Tour
Stop Eight:
West Confederate Avenue

After leaving STOP SEVEN continue north past Hummelbaugh's farm lane past the Copse of Trees and the Angle. Exit the park as you did earlier, except this time turn right, north, on Steinwehr Avenue instead of left. Travel one-quarter mile to the first intersection, then turn left onto Washington Street. Follow that avenue one-half mile to West Middle Street and turn left again. As you head west you will travel approximately three-quarters of a mile to West Confederate Avenue. Turn left. You are now on Seminary Ridge.

West Confederate Avenue was a road at the time of battle. Used as a cutoff between the Fairfield (Hagerstown) Road and present day Millerstown Road, it once connected with the Black Horse Tavern Road near Pitzer's Schoolhouse and Woods, where the former road crossed Willoughby Run. In all likelihood, Wilcox's and Lang's men used one of these rural lanes to gain their jumping off point, with Wilcox's Alabamans skirmishing with Berdan's Sharpshooters and the 3rd Maine Volunteers east of where their markers are located, off West Confederate Avenue in the wooded area to the west.

We will, however, pull off the road long before those markers are reached. To see where Lang's Floridians first deployed, we must stop just south of Spangler's Woods near the monument dedicated to Perry's (Lang's) Florida Brigade. After visiting that monument, walk beyond it to the east so that you can better see the fields this brigade crossed. Looking north, beyond Spangler's house, it is evident that this brigade deployed north of the farmyard, screened by the Emmitsburg Road Rise and unseen by Turnbull, Seeley, or any other body of Federal soldiers east of the Emmitsburg Road. They, however, were seen and fired upon by advanced skirmishers from Carr's brigade who held the first rise west of Spangler's Woods.

Advancing out of the woods, Lang's Floridians swept aside these skirmishers as they topped that first rise, only to come under fire from Turnbull's five Napoleons engaging from near the Rogers house. Within moments of the lieutenant's opening, Weir's five smoothbores opened as well from Cemetery Ridge (STOP THREE) as directed by Gibbon. Continuing east, Lang's men dropped into the center swale, then ascended the next rise where a rail fence paralleled its crest, offering Carr's skirmishers slight protection. After taking that rail fence, they were met by an increased spattering of musketry from more Federals behind another rail fence not 50 yards distant. This is the rise where Captain Ransom was wounded and where Turnbull's battery first opened with canister.

Return to West Confederate Avenue, then walk or drive south, approximately 300 yards, to the State of Alabama monument. After visiting the Alabama monument and Wilcox's brigade plaque, continue east to the crest of the next rise. You are standing above the swale where Kemper's brigade lay on July Third and where Wilcox's Alabamans kicked off their

July Second attack.

Although history has them stepping over the stone wall east of West Confederate Avenue, the short walk you have just taken should make clear that the brigade was not seriously engaged by artillery from Seeley's gunners until they crested the rise to your front. Note the Staub house to your right, 400 yards distant. Two Confederate batteries were firing eastward between you and that farmhouse, and Barksdale's skirmishers were to your right front. Because of the terrain's natural features, Barksdale's left wing, near the Millerstown Road, was actually east of you.

There were enormous gaps already between both Wilcox's flanks and those of Lang and Barksdale. His brigade was already isolated, with both flanks in the air. Because the rise you are on runs from west-northwest to east-southeast, when you advance you will be heading east-northeast, directly toward Cemetery Hill in the distance. Between that hill and you lay the Spangler and Klingle farms with Plum Run and Cemetery Ridge beyond.

When Wilcox began his attack, the Mississippians to your right had already begun theirs. Moving due east, Barksdale did as ordered; he pivoted, or wheeled, due north, up the Emmitsburg Road. Wilcox's Alabamans followed suit, advancing in echelon, their right flank beyond Barksdale's left, which was now engaged along the Emmitsburg Road Rise. Hit hard by the 12th New Jersey Volunteers, Wilcox's advance was slowed even more when Seeley's Napoleons raked his line at near perfect right-front enfilade. That, however, ended when Wilcox's Alabamians dropped into the swale west of the rise.

Walk back to your car and drive south to the State of Mississippi Monument. The location of this monument does not correspond accurately with Barksdale's Mississippi Brigade. Although his left flank was north of Millerstown Road, the bulk of his brigade was south of it. Your visit offers you a good view, however, of the Emmitsburg Road Rise and South Cemetery Ridge, with Plum Run Ravine in between. Note the tall trees beyond the Klingle house, north of United States Avenue. That is Plum Run Ravine. Those trees were not there at the time of battle, thus no one on either side had any inkling of the hollow in that terrain.

Walk back to your car and drive south, leaving STOP EIGHT and head to STOP NINE, the last in our tour. Here we will point out exactly why Generals Kershaw and Semmes could not wheel their brigades up the Emmitsburg Road as had Barksdale.

Driving and Walking Tour
Stop Nine:
The Peach Orchard

For a full appreciation of the terrain over which Barksdale advanced, and to get something of a bird's eye view of South Cemetery Ridge, a visit to the Peach Orchard is necessary. After leaving STOP EIGHT, turn left onto Millerstown Road. This will take you past the Warfield and Staub homesteads, both marked by plaques on the buildings. Barksdale's brigade straddled the Millerstown road with his right wing well south of it. He began his wheel to the north shortly after passing these homes. This brought his right flank regiment, the 21st Mississippi, heading directly toward the present day Millerstown–Emmitsburg Roads intersection at what is referred to as an oblique.

When the 21st Mississippi wheeled half-left that placed the regiment's right flank in the air. Kershaw's South Carolinians, who were south of the 21st, stepped off in alignment with the brigades from Hood's division who were in turn south of them. Kershaw's orders were simple. He was to come in on the right of Barksdale and advance up the Emmitsburg Road, attacking what was then thought to be the Federal left flank. In turn, Semmes's Georgians following in reserve would support his brigade. Wofford's Georgians were on the left of Semmes, following Barksdale.

The attack plan unraveled quickly. The first reason was that the Emmitsburg Road Rise was occupied in force by Sickles's Third Corps, which was not the case when the plans were made; but there was another reason why this attack could not go forward as planned.

Two man-made obstacles and one natural impediment thwarted Kershaw from the outset—the two plank fences paralleling the Emmitsburg Road and a deep ravine, unknown to the Confederates. Kershaw's brigade was initially hammered at near point blank range by case, solid shot, shell, and canister, from six smoothbores and six rifled cannon engaging from the Sherfy Peach Orchard, and by musketry from several Federal regiments, all from the relative safety north of the ravine Kershaw knew nothing about. Housing the headwaters of the west branch of Plum Run (proper), it became an immediate impediment. With Barksdale north of it and Kershaw south of it, a gap naturally opened when the latter's brigade was forced to redirect its advance after its initial attack was repulsed following its half-wheel. Kershaw had to pull back and then redirect his advance due east, moving away from Barksdale, who was headed north.

Cross over the Emmitsburg Road onto Wheatfield Road, and drive approximately 200 yards east to Birney Avenue, a one-way lane. Turn right. From Birney Avenue you can view the Sherfy Peach Orchard if you choose not to stop. Continue around Birney Avenue toward the 2nd New Hampshire Monument located near the intersection of Birney Avenue and Emmitsburg Road. This is STOP NINE. It is well defined because the ravine housing the west branch of Plum Run is to your immediate left as you face west.

Get out of your car and walk to the edge of that ravine. The famous Rose house and the foundation to the barn will be to your left and front, south of the ravine. This is the farm to which Kershaw withdrew and regrouped after being initially repulsed, after the left and center of his line came upon the ravine. Walk to the intersection west of you, toward the monument to the 68th Pennsylvania Infantry. Stand at that regiment's marker and scan the terrain west of the Emmitsburg Road. Note the depression in the ground; Barksdale was north of that.

From the intersection, look back in the direction of the Wheatfield Road—Birney Avenue intersection. Though it is only a little distance away, you cannot see it! Walk uphill to the center of the Peach Orchard. Once you reach the crest, everything opens up before you, a full and commanding vista, although at that day and time, it was encased in smoke and chaos. From his position in the lower ground south of the ravine, Kershaw could not witness Barksdale's move up the Emmitsburg Road, at least not until his brigade took the Stony Hill.

Looking toward Cemetery Ridge, and the Pennsylvania State Monument's dome a mile to the northeast, you can see that during the battle that distant area was meaningless. It may not even have been visible due to the engulfing smoke, confusion of battle, and simply because troops in combat focus on their immediate front and not some unknown low-lying ridge a mile away. Like Kershaw south of the Peach Orchard, Barksdale, who possibly could see that low ridge from near the Staub and Warfield homes, quickly lost all sense of direction once his brigade became embroiled below the crest of the Emmitsburg Road Rise.

The detaching of the 21st Mississippi was Barksdale's undoing. From the crest where you are standing, you can see the ground to the north and east, but standing in the Sherfy farmyard you cannot. To this day, there is no clear explanation of why Wofford continued due east once his brigade made contact with the Emmitsburg Road. Instead of following Barksdale north, it is very possible that Wofford simply aligned on the detached 21st Mississippi, which by then was directing its attack due east up the Trostle Farm Lane. That regiment's redirection in all probability rerouted Wofford's support away from Barksdale. Whatever the case, Barksdale entered the Plum Run Ravine basically unsupported on his right, his right flank regiment detached, and with no reinforcements to count on.

Looking north you will clearly see what Barksdale had to contend with and how that brigade alone almost did the impossible. Now look toward the Sherfy buildings toward United States Avenue and imagine Wilcox's Alabamans coming in, advancing on an already disorganized Third Corps line that was improperly placed to begin with. Look at the Klingle farm noting how Seeley was isolated on the crest of the rise. Had you been manning one of his guns you would have been subjected to duel flank enfilade as well as frontal fire. Imagine the huge Sherfy peach orchard and the terror and carnage within.

Now scan the entire field from Millerstown Road west, then north to Spangler's farm and beyond. Look east past the Emmitsburg Road to Cemetery Ridge. Focus on the guns planted along Hancock Avenue near where Willard's men counter-charged. Note the compactness of this battle-field where so many thousands of men engaged in a death struggle.

Between the trees and the rise where you stand, look to the tall trees standing in the hollow made sacred by several thousand men who crossed bayonets and fired almost blindly into foes but 10 feet away. Within that shallow ravine are markers that cry out for every officer and man from both armies. Here we advanced, here we stood, and here we died. This was the turning point, July Second, 1863, not only of the battle but, possibly, of the entire war.

Endnotes

Prologue

[1] *The War of the Rebellion: A Compilation of the Official Records of the Union and Confederate Armies*, 128 volumes in 4 series (Washington: U.S. Government Printing Office, 1889), series 1, vol. 27, pt. 1, 474. See circular dated July 7, 1863. (Hereafter cited as *OR*. All excerpts are from this Series, Volume, and Part unless otherwise indicated.)

[2] Edwin B. Coddington, *The Gettysburg Campaign: A Study in Command* (New York: Charles Scribner's Sons, 1968), 423 (Hereafter cited as *The Gettysburg Campaign*).

[3] William Lochren, "The First Minnesota at Gettysburg," *Glimpses of the Nation's Struggle*, Minnesota Commandery, Military Order of the Loyal Legion of the United States, vol. 3 (1893), 42-56.

[4] Robert W. Meinhard, "The First Minnesota At Gettysburg," *Gettysburg Magazine* 5 (1991), 81 (Hereafter referred to as *GBM*) (see also note 19).

Chapter 1

[1] These woods, often referred to as Patterson's Woods, belonged to Sarah Patterson and separated the Schriber and Patterson farms.

[2] *OR*, 459. Willard was detached from the 14th Indiana

to command the Pioneer Corps. The Second Corps Pioneers must have arrived about 6:00 A.M. in order to clear fences belonging to Jacob Hummelbaugh and Peter Frey. All times represented here are either given by participants or developed from the events themselves. Two eyewitnesses to the same event may report it as happening at significantly different times – one may report it as occurring at 4:00 P.M., another at 6:00 P.M. In all such cases we are concerned more with when events occur relative to each other, which can be determined, than from the absolute time of the events, which cannot.

[3]David Shultz & David Wieck: *Federal Artillery at Gettysburg: A Comprehensive Study.* (Forthcoming) see also *OR*, 872.

[4]*OR*, 407. Maj. Leman W. Bradley, commanding the 64th New York Infantry, Fourth Brigade, First Division, in rear of Hays, recalled, "At 4:10 A.M. we moved about 1 mile to the front, and at 5:45 A.M. halted in a wood."

[5]*Ibid.,* Bradley left a very accurate account of his movements and their times.

[6]Hancock's parking of Ransom's ammunition train was the spark that ignited bitter resentment between Generals Hunt and Hancock. Their disagreement would span two decades, ending only upon Hancock's premature death.

[7]Colonel Bradley also remembered, "at 6:00 we were marched with the brigade out of the woods across the Taneytown Road." Although Bradley commanded a regiment in Caldwell's First Division, which arrived last in the woods, his accuracy concerning time can be applied to the arrival of

the entire Second Corps.

[8]Today's Artillery Ridge. This ridge parallels Cemetery Ridge at virtually the same height, save Powers' Hill, supporting Baltimore Pike from the Taneytown Road. Four distinct routes, plus numerous secondary lanes, twisted through this ridge connecting the throughways. It took approximately eight minutes on horseback, and about 20 on foot to traverse the ridge.

[9]Careerist: advancing one's career often at the cost of one's integrity. The gathering of officers allegedly included Generals Hancock, Gibbon, Hays, Doubleday, Newton, Hunt, and Tyler. (Henry Hunt to Dunbar Ransom, Fort Hamilton, N.Y., August 21, 1872. Hunt Papers Box 16, General Correspondence. Washington, D.C., Library of Congress [Hereafter cited as LC]).

[10]The old Fairfield Crossroad was a rural wagon road that is referred to today as the Wheatfield Road.

[11]*OR*, 368-370. It was Hancock who initially instructed Geary to send men to Little Round Top on July First, indicating that Hancock knew the importance of gaining and controlling the length of Cemetery Ridge.

Chapter 2

[1]Captain Willard's Pioneers opened an avenue by dismantling several hundred yards of rail fence. See William A. Frassanito, *Gettysburg: A Journey In Time* (New York: Charles Scribner's Sons, 1975), 144. Note the missing rail fencing

along the length of the Taneytown Road. Military General Orders prohibited soldiers from dismantling rail, or private fences that were intact. This close to army headquarters, it is doubtful that foragers would display such conduct. It is more likely foragers used the already dismantled rails for firewood.

[2]In 1863 the famous Copse of Trees was nothing more then a small twisted grove of a few small oaks (12–15 feet high) and secondary growth junk timber and was used as a dumping ground, or junk yard, for rocks, boulders, probably old wood and discarded farm equipment, etc. Gibbon actually detailed men to Cushing's front to clear a field of fire through the rubble and slashing (junk second growth). Another copse of trees east of and above Taneytown Road (across from the present-day Visitor's Center) on the highest point of Cemetery Hill was much larger and could be seen from as far south as the Warfield house. There are more references to the "Big Gray Stone House" (Peter Frey residence) by the soldiers than to the Copse of Trees.

[3]Dunbar Ransom to Henry Hunt, July 10th, 1863, LC. Ransom recalled the time and events: "I am grateful for your kind consideration about my injury. Although serious it causes me no discomfort. I heard you also had been wounded and am pleased to hear you are not. Your request inquiring, what time Gen. Hancock's column crossed over the ridge I am not sure. I do recall having looked at my watch when Gen. Hays and his staff rode by. It was nearly 6:30 A.M. After what seemed an hour you asked again about the time, and it was only 7:00. I do not think Gen. Hays's column had completely passed

over. You stayed but a few moments when the captain [Hazard presumably] commanding Hancock's artillery approached. Although I did not hear your conversation I do recall you told him it was 7:00 A.M." Ransom places Hays's arrival at about 6:30 A.M. Time varies from regiment to regiment as to their arrival. Several reported arriving as early as 4:30 A.M. while others in the same brigade reported arriving at 8:30 A.M. Ransom's time seems to fit with Second Corps reveille being called at 4:30 A.M. when in bivouac east of Little Round Top.

[4]Edward Warner to Henry Hunt, July 6, 1863, LC. Willard was commissioned a first lieutenant in the regular army at the outset of war. After being promoted to captain, Willard rapidly advanced in rank, jumping to brevet colonel of volunteers after receiving command of the newly organized 125th New York on August 15th, 1862.

Colonel Warner wrote, "Finding the road [Taneytown] closed to traffic I thought it best to bring at least two batteries forward immediately. Not knowing where Capt. Hazard was I assumed responsibility and in your name removed them from the Second Division [Gibbon]. I sent Capt. Craig to Gen. Gibbon to inform him of my intentions. They were to report to you at headquarters [Leister House, Army Headquarters] with the guns. I turned off the road near the [Peter Frey] stone house passing through the lane running perpendicular to the ridge. Not finding you I reported to Gen. Hays who took possession of the guns."

[5]USGS, Map 39077–G2–TF–024. See also Bachelder Map dated 1872 titled "July Second."

[6]David Shultz & Richard Rollins, "Measuring Pickett's Charge," *GBM* 17 (1997), 108–116. (Hereafter cited *as* "Measuring Pickett's Charge.") These distance are exact, measured with a GPS verified by the USGS, Map 39077–G2–TF–024.

[7]Elwood Christ, *The Struggle for the Bliss Farm at Gettysburg,* (Baltimore: Butternut and Blue, 1994)*,* 15–16.

[8]Bryan's name was spelled with a "y" when he filed his claim against the government in 1863. The authors believe the file was written out by someone other than Bryan, a clerk perhaps, and that he, Bryan, was illiterate. The name could be Brian but the fact remains it is signed Bryan on the official document.

[9]"Measuring Pickett's Charge," 108–116.

Chapter 3

[1]*Struggle for the Bliss Farm,* 15–16. See also: New York Monuments Commission for the Battlefields of Gettysburg and Chattanooga, *New York at Gettysburg: Final Report on the Battlefield of Gettysburg*, 3 vols. (Albany: Lyon Company Printers, 1900), 2:800. (Hereafter referred to as *NYaGB*.)

[2]*Ibid.*

[3]Other Second Corps members bestowed the unflattering moniker "Harpers Ferry Cowards" upon the brigade. The brigade joined the Second Corps after being paroled.

⁴John W. Busey and David G. Martin, *Regimental Strengths and Losses at Gettysburg,* (Hightstown, N.J: Longstreet House. 1986), 44 and 203 (Hereafter cited as *Strengths & Losses*). See, also, Edmund J. Raus Jr., *A Generation on the March - The Union Army at Gettysburg,* (Lynchburg, Va.: H. E. Howard, Inc. 1987), 58. (Hereafter cited as *Union Army at Gettysburg.*)

⁵Personal Military and Pension Records of C. D. MacDougall. (Washington, D.C., NNRG-NA). See also *The Union Army at Gettysburg,* 77. Hildebrandt and MacDougall openly disliked each other. The latter thought Hildebrant a braggart and contemptible bastard.

⁶*Ibid.* See also *The Union Army at Gettysburg,* 58. Capt. Aaron P. Seeley of the 111th New York recalled, "We lay in this position until 5 P.M. most of the afternoon under a furious shelling from the enemy."

⁷Richardson to Bachelder, June 18, 1867, included in David L. Ladd and Audrey J. Ladd, *The Bachelder Papers: Gettysburg in Their Own Words,* 3 vols. (Dayton, Ohio: Morningside, 1995), 1:315. (Hereafter cited as *BP.*) Capt. Charles Richardson, 126th New York, watched and later wrote, "Here a lively skirmish took place, and the enemy's reinforcements to their line, coming from the northwest [McMillan Woods] through the orchard close to the barn, began to drive back the 39th New York, but, Gen. Alex Hays, accompanied by his adjutant general and the division flag dashed down on horseback to the line, rallied the men under a shower of bullets, reestablished the line and rode back unharmed."

[8]*Ibid.*. 319. Richardson described Hays's flag as "plain white square with blue trefoil."

[9] *NyaGB*, 2:800.

[10]*BP,* 2:300. MacDougall wrote that "the two companies were detailed as skirmishers not long after arriving." See also, *The Struggle for the Bliss Farm*, 19.

Chapter 4

[1]*OR*, 442. Col. Arthur F. Devereux, commanding the 19th Massachusetts recalled:

"At daybreak of the 2nd we marched to the front, this division forming in columns of regiment by brigade on the right of the road, with its front toward the right of the position held by our army [they were fronting north]."

Chapter 5

[1]USGS, Map 39077–G2–TF–024.

[2]The Confederate guns ranged from the McMillan Woods south to Spangler's Woods on South Seminary Ridge. Most likely these guns belonged to Brander, Zimmerman, Marye, Wingfield, and Ross. They outnumbered Batteries A and B, 20 guns to 12.

[3]For information concerning Confederate Artillery see Richard Rollins's three-piece essay titled *"The Guns Of*

Gettysburg," North & South Magazine. Volume 3, Issues No. 2, 3, & 4. (Tollhouse, Ca.: North & South Publications. 2000.) It should be noted that the Emmitsburg Road Rise near the Klingle House and Sherfy Peach Orchard Rise is higher than South Cemetery Ridge. Capt. Judson Clark commanding, Battery B, 1st New Jersey Light, Third Corps Artillery Brigade, knew this and noted it.

[4]According to General Harrow, "the division arrived upon the battle-field on the morning of the 2nd, and was ordered into position by Brig. Gen. John Gibbon, as follows: The Second Brigade [Webb]——occupied the right of the division——. The Third Brigade [Hall] connected with the left of Gen. Webb's brigade, and continued the line in the direction of Round Top Mountain to the left, their two brigades covering a front of 500 yards. The First Brigade, my own command, was placed in reserve 100 yards in rear of the Second [Webb] and Third [Hall] Brigades and opposite the center of the line." *OR,* 419.

[5]*Measuring Pickett's Charge.* 108–116.

[6]*Ibid.* See also: Personal Military and Pension Records of Francis E. Heath. (Washington, D.C., NNRG-NA). Born in Belfast, Maine, February 28th, 1838, Heath grew up in an abolitionist environment and detested the social system that supported slavery. Educated in the public school system he graduated with honors from Waterville College. Well organized and sensible, he found immediate employment as an Accountant-Clerk in the mercantile trade where his keen business sense quickly led him to a management position with

a dry goods distribution company. Heath left that post at the outbreak of war and was commissioned second lieutenant in the 3rd Regiment Maine Volunteer Infantry. He resigned that commission to become lieutenant colonel of the 19th Maine on August 25, 1862. Heath would lead a well-rounded public life after the war, serving several terms in the Maine State Legislature.

[7]Though Heath could not know it, this encounter with Hancock's Second Corps threw Stuart's timetable disastrously out of whack. Stuart, who planned to and ultimately did ride completely around the Army of the Potomac, was so delayed by his encounter with the Second Corps that he would not be available to Lee until late in the afternoon of July Second.

[8]John Day Smith, *The History of the Nineteenth Regiment of Maine Volunteers Infantry, 1862-1865* (Minneapolis, Minn.: Great Western Printing Company, 1909), 58 (Hereafter referred to as *19th Maine*). See also *OR*, Vol. 27, Pt. 2, 692

[9]*NyaGB*, 2:.800.

[10]*19th Maine,* 20.

Chapter 6

[1]The 15th Massachusetts continued north on the Taneytown Road, moving onto the ridge via the Peter Frey farm. It is clear that that column was stopped somewhere near the road because they were the last of Harrow's regiments to arrive.

[2]*OR*, Pt. 2, 423 and 426.

[3]The 1st Minnesota numbered 330 men at Gettysburg, Colvill and 29 officers included. This included Companies C and L. Company C was detached on the night of July First as Provost Guards. Company L—the 2nd Minnesota Sharpshooters—was detached for skirmishing duties before the 1st Minnesota was ordered forward. After detaching these two companies, the regiment consisted of 262 officers and men.

[4]*OR*, 424. Capt. Henry C. Coats, later to command the battery and record the official report, noted without excitement, "We remained under a severe artillery fire, but were not actively engaged until about 5:00 P.M."

[5]So-called because there was a blacksmith shop operating on that portion of the Fairfield Crossroad. The property Caldwell's division occupied was near the farm belonging to Sarah Patterson, sister of William Patterson, whose property was occupied by Hays's division one-quarter mile further north. Sarah's farm was separated from William's by the Michael Fry and Jacob Swiser farms, which were occupied by portions of Hays, Gibbons, and Caldwell's divisions, from left to right facing east. The woods Caldwell's division occupied were just north of Sarah's house directly east of and across the Taneytown Road from the Patterson Woods with Cemetery Ridge less then 300 yards distant.

[6]*OR,* 386. Col. Patrick Kelly, commanding the 68th New York Infantry remembered, "Arriving on the heights near the village, and in view of of the enemy's pickets, we took a position in two lines on the right of the First Brigade, stacked arms, and allowed the men to rest."

[7]Capt. James M. Rorty would not assume command of Battery B until later that day.

[8]*OR,* 379. Caldwell reported, "My command arrived on the field of battle on the morning of July Second, and was placed in position by General Hancock on the left of the Second (Gibbon's) Division, in columns of brigade."

Chapter 7

[1]*The Struggle For The Bliss Farm At Gettysburg*, 15.

[2]Referred to today as Houck's Ridge.

[3]The batteries were Clark: 1st New Jersey, Battery B and Bucklyn: 1st Rhode Island, Battery E.

[4]*OR,* 873. Tyler states that he sent the regulars to the ridge near army headquarters.

[5]Morgan to Hunt. June 5, 1876, LC. Morgan recalled: "Passing the stone [Frey] house we found Gen. Caldwell in conversation with his staff. On Hancock's request he accompanied us to the crest where we dismounted in the orchard near your headquarters [Hummelbaugh barn]. Gen. Hancock explained to him what had to be done adding you would see to the artillery. I believe you offered Colonel [Capt. at that time] Ransom's batteries from the regular reserves."

[6]Caldwell had initially offered one of his brigades to support Gibbon's regiments on the Emmitsburg Road. They had moved but a short distance before being recalled for the move south.

Chapter 8

[1]Evan Thomas & Gulian Weir Personal Military and Pension Records (NNRA-AGO. Washington, D.C.). Lieutenant Weir's brother Henry served on the staff of Brig. Gen. David M. Gregg, commander of the Army of the Potomac's Second Cavalry Division. Henry C. Weir was awarded a Medal of Honor for valor at the June 24, 1864 Battle of Samaria Church for saving General Gregg from being captured. Obviously, courage and valor ran deep in the Weir family.

[2]U.S. Geological Survey Satellite Image: Gettysburg: 39077-G2-TF-024 overlaid with the Bachelder July Second map, dated 1876.

[3]*Ibid.* These distance are exact, measured with a GPS verified by the USGS, Map 39077–G2–TF–024.

[4]Hunt encountered Weir on the crest after having returned from visiting Sickles. After asking Weir where he was parked, Hunt told him to stay put, obviously forgetting he had already detached him to the Second Corps. Later in the day, when Hunt went looking for batteries to bolster McGilvery's line, he sent Colonel Warner in search for Weir and Thomas, who he thought were near Caldwell.

[5]U.S. Geological Survey Satellite Image: Gettysburg: 39077-G2-TF-024.

Chapter 9

[1]This was Hiram Berdan's 1st U.S. Sharpshooters and Col. Moses Lakeman's 3rd Maine Infantry engaging Wilcox's advance guard near the Pitzer Schoolhouse.

[2]According to Harrow, that order was relayed to him directly from Gibbon and in turn, according to Heath, relayed to the 19th Maine by Capt. John P. Blinn, Harrow's assistant adjutant-general. Blinn, a United States Volunteer, was mortally wounded July Third while leading reinforcements back to the stone wall during Pickett's Charge. *OR*, 421.

[3]John Smith, the 19th Maine historian, recalled, "About five [2:00 PM] o'clock the First Minnesota was taken from the Brigade and conducted a short distance to the left, to support Battery C, Fourth United States Artillery." Smith. *Nineteenth Maine,* 69.

[4]*OR*, 419. Colonel Harrow wrote: "The First Minnesota Volunteers, Colonel Colvill commanding, by the direction of General Gibbon, were moved from their original position in the rear, to the left of a battery commanded by Lieutenant Thomas, and stationed on the high ground a short distance to the left of the division line of battle. The Nineteenth Maine Volunteers, Colonel Heath commanding, moved to the left front of the division line, and placed in position to the right of a battery commanded by Lieutenant [Captain] Brown."

[5]Smith wrote, "That left the Nineteenth Maine particularly alone on that particular part of the field it then

occupied." Smith, *Nineteenth Maine*, 69.

[6]There is a possibility Caldwell was the "I will see what I can do" help that Meade promised Sickles The reason Brown's Rhode Island Battery was moved forward was because two of Hall's regiments, the 19th Massachusetts and 42nd New York, which had been covering that area, had been sent south to Humphreys.

[7]U.S. Geological Survey Satellite Image: Gettysburg: 39077-G2-TF-024.

Chapter 10

[1]Patterson's seven cannons.

[2]Ransom was out of the fight, for the moment. He reported to a field hospital to have his wound examined. It was probed, the ball extracted, and the wound dressed and bandaged. After a night's rest, the captain reported to General Tyler for duty the next morning.

[3]Gulian Weir to Hunt. Governor Island, New York Harbor, October, 23, 1880. Hunt Papers, Box 14, Military Correspondences (Washington, D.C., Library of Congress).

[4]*OR,* 880. See also Shultz, "Gulian V. Weir's 5th United States Artillery, Battery C," *GBM,* Issue 18, 83.

[5]Capt. George E. Randolph to Bachelder, Central City, Co., March 1866. See *BP* Vol. 1, 240. See also John Bigelow, Jr., *The Peach Orchard, Gettysburg, July 2, 1863* (Minneapolis, 1910), 12.

⁶*OR*, 880. Wilcox's Alabama Brigade's on Barksdale's left wing and Lang's Florida Brigade to their left-rear.

⁷Charles Richardson Papers, *Marches, Engagements of the 126th N.Y. Vols.,* (Canandaigua, N.Y.: Ontario County Historical Society, n.p.) Letter from Sweet to Richardson, September, 4, 1895. See also: Hancock's testimony before the Joint Committee on the Conduct of the War of the U.S. Congress, *Report of the Joint Committee on the Conduct of the War.* (Washington, D.C. LC, 1865), 406. (Hereafter cited as *JCCW.*) See also: Shultz. *GBM*, Issue 18, 83.

⁸Hancock. *JCCW*, 1865, p 406 see also: *GBM*, Issue 18, 83

Chapter 11

¹Richardson to Bachelder, May 6, 1868. *BP*, 1:338-339. Colonel Richardson states that the brigade was sent south at approximately 5:00 P.M.

²Letter from Sweet to Richardson, dated September, 4, 1895.

³Fixed Prolonge: The prolonge [rope] is used with field-pieces to attach the gun to its limber when firing in retreat, or advancing, instead of limbering up; for the same purpose in crossing ditches, for slinging a piece to a limber; for righting carriages when upset, and for various other purposes. The drag rope may be substituted for that of the prolonge if necessary. Gibbon, *The Artillerist's Manual*, 297.

[4]*OR*, 883. Referred to as Pettit's battery, Sheldon was placed on the right of the 6th Maine Light [Dow], straddling the narrow Trostle Lane north of the Weikert Farm.

[5]Hancock's testimony, *JCCW,* 406. See also Shultz, *GBM*, Issue 18, 83-85. See also *OR*, 576–7.

[6]Luckily for Weir, there was another tempting prize closer to Wright then Battery C, that being Brown's Rhode Island Light, Battery B. Most of Wright's Georgians made for that battery. There is no further word of Private Wells.

Chapter 12

[1]Smith, *History of the 19th Maine,* 70. The actual distance was nearer 600 yards.

[2]Turnbull to Hunt, July, 1863,.Hunt papers. See also *GBM*, Issue 18, 84. This document appears to be Turnbull's unpublished and supposedly lost official report on the Battle of Gettysburg. Although barely legible, it mentions critical points in the battle which are already well documented. See also *GBM*, Issue 18, 83.

[3]Seeley had dismissed all but two of his caissons before the Emmitsburg Road position had collapsed

[4]*BP*, 3:1651. See also *GBM*, Issue 18, 84.

[5]Smith, *History of the 19th Maine,* 70.

[6]*OR,* 442–443.

[7]*Ibid.*

[8]Smith, *History of the 19th Maine,* 71 and 76. This

officer was later falsely alleged to be General Humphreys himself. Although the incident certainly took place, there is no evidence to substantiate that it was the general. As stated in *The History of the 19th Maine,* "This fiction really never happened until after the general's death, December 27,1883."

[9]*Ibid.* Turnbull fired spherical case because he had used most of his canister during the prolonge from the Emmitsburg Road. The lieutenant had dispatched a courier to bring back a caisson limber with ammunition.

Chapter 13

[1]Smith, *History of the 19th Maine*, 71.

[2]Turnbull to Hunt, July, 1863, Hunt papers. See, also, Ladd & Sauers. *BP.* 1:231 and 284. See also *OR,* 190, 237, 534, and 878.

[3]Shultz. *GBM*, Issue 18, 86.

[4]How many rounds were fired prior to his death is not known. Personal Military Records of Manning Livingston (Washington, D.C., NNRG – NA).

[5]Hancock's testimony, *JCCW*, 406.

[6]Colvill to Bachelder, June 9th, 1866, *BP*, 1:257.

[7]Meinhard. *GBM*, Issue 5. Alfred Carpenter Letter, dated July Third, 1863, copy in files in GNMP archives.

[8]*OR*, 541

[9]*Ibid.*, 541 and 443.

[10]*Ibid.*, 371.

[11]*Ibid.*

[12]*Ibid.*, 472

[13]As distinct from the crest of the ridge, the military crest is where a defending line on a hill or ridge has a field of fire all the way to the base, leaving no blind pockets or concealed avenues of approach. Similarly, when placing artillery, it was important not to silhouette the guns on the crest but rather use it to conceal the battery's position, making it harder to target. Thomas's position was a splendid example of this; Arnold's and Cushing's were not.

[14]*Ibid.* It is evident from Bull's statement that Willard had no idea the ridge descended into Plum Run to the depth it did.

[15]*Ibid.*, 474.

[16]*Ibid.* See also: MacDougall to Charles Richardson, June 30, 1886, GNMP archives.

[17]*OR*, 475.

[18]Personal Military Records of George Bently & James Riddle, 3rd Regiment U.S. Light Artillery, Battery K. (Washington, D.C. NNRG – NA).

[19]Smith, *History of the 19th Maine.*, 72.

[20]*Ibid.*

[21]*OR*, 559

[22]Shultz. *GBM*, Issue 18, 86.

[23]*Ibid.*

[24]*Ibid.*

[25]*OR.*, Pt. 2, 631.

[26]Turnbull to Hunt, July 1863, Hunt Papers; see, also,

Smith, *History of the 19th Maine*, 71.

Chapter 14

[1]Unbeknownst to Hancock, Willard's 125th and 126th NY regiments had already stopped the far right of Wilcox's advance and were then engaging Barksdale. See also: *BP*, 1:340.

[2]*OR*, 475.

Chapter 15

[1] Dr. Robert W. Meinhard. GBM, Issue Five, July, 1991. *"No Soldiers Ever Displayed Grander Heroism" The First Minnesota at Gettysburg.* GBM 5, July 1991, 79-88. Alfred Carpenter Letter, dated July 3, 1863 (copy in GNMP archives).

[2] Hancock to Bachelder, November 7, 1885. *BP. Vol. II.* p. 1135

[3] Ibid. See also: Colvill to Bachelder. Letter dated June 9th, 1866. *BP, 1,* 257

[4] Glen Tucker. *Hancock the Superb* (Indianapolis, Bobbs-Merril Company, 1958). 144-145. see also John D. Imhof. *Gettysburg Day Two: A Study In Maps* (Baltimore, Butternut and Blue. 1999]. 180-182 See Map 35 denoting the line of Brewster reforming.

[5] The batteries were as follows, Seeley [James] - Two

Napoleons, Dow - Four Napoleons, Sheldon - Four 10-Pdr Parrotts, Thompson -Three 3-Inch Ordnance Rifles, Phillips - Four 3-Inch Ordnance Rifles, Clark - Three-10-Pdr Parrots, Watson - Four 10-Pdr Parrotts, and Bigelow - Six Napoleons. Of these 30 guns 24 were engaged. Clark and Seeley never opened. Two of these batteries, 10 guns total, were overrun before the ridge was solidified. Never the less, they helped slow down Barksdale's advance. See also 1990 U.S Geological Survey Satellite Image: Map 39077-G2-TF-024, Gettysburg..

[6] Meinhard. *GBM* 5, 82.

[7] Ibid. See also Carpenter letter dated July 3, 1863 GNMP archives.

[8] Although Humphreys reformed command fired toward the gap most of these men engaged were from 300-400 yards away, aiming down the slope, their rounds mostly sailing overhead of the approaching Wilcox.

[9] Colvill to Bachelder. June 9, 1866. *BP, I.* 257

[10] *Ibid.*

[11] Anne A Hage, "The Battle of Gettysburg as Seen by Minnesota Soldiers," *Minnesota History 38* (June 1963); 256.

[12] U.S. Geological Survey Satellite Image: Gettysburg: 39077-G2-TF-024, 1990. See also Bachelder Map dated 1876.

[13] In fairness, these were men from a variety of units who had found the courage to turn and fight, but they were not with their comrades or their regular officers. It would have been very difficult for them to put together an organized advance.

[14] Turnbull to Hunt, July 1863, Hunt Papers, L.C. The line to the left could have been either the 1st Minnesota or that

belonging to Humphreys.

Chapter 16

¹*OR*, Pt. 2. 618.

²*Ibid.* See also U.S. Geological Survey Satellite Image 39077-G2-TF-024, 1990, and Bachelder Map, July Second Field, 1876.

³*Ibid.* 619. Colonel Forney had received flesh wounds in the arm and chest prior to having his right arm shattered. Personal Military Records of William H. Forney, CSA. (National Archives: NNRG-NA, Washington, D.C.)

⁴*Ibid.*

⁵U.S. Geological Survey Satellite Image: Map 39077-G2-TF-024, 1990 overlaid using Bachelder Map dated 1876.

⁶*OR*, 425. See also Busey, *These Honored Dead*, 85; Busey and Martin, *Regimental Strengths,* 185–186; R. I. Holcombe, *History of the First Regiment Minnesota Volunteer Infantry* (Stillwater: Easton & Masterman, 1916),. 343–345 (hereafter cited as Holcombe).

⁷Smith, *History of the 19th Maine*, 57.

⁸*OR*, Pt. 2, 631–632.

⁹*Ibid.*

¹⁰*OR*, 559.

¹¹*Ibid.* Veterans from the 19th Maine would dispute Brewster's claim long into the 20th century. They also challenged Brewster, claiming it was the 19th Maine who recaptured Turnbull's battery.

¹²*OR*, Pt. 2, 632.

Chapter 17

¹*OR*, 804.

²*Ibid.*, 805.

³This was the same fire Willard's brigade had run into as they advanced.

⁴Men from the 1st Maryland turned over possession of the four Napoleons belonging to Capt. John Bigelow's 9th Massachusetts to the 150th New York, who returned them to Colonel McGilvery after dark.

Chapter 18

¹Stone had been wounded on July 1.

²By sending Rorty back to his unit, Hancock gained at least one battery commander loyal to him. Because Capt. John Hazard had not yet been officially commissioned a captain, Rorty, who had been commissioned, therefore had a good chance of gaining control of the Second Corps' Artillery Brigade. Hancock knew this and made his move. For reasons not yet known, the usually feisty Sheldon, a Hunt loyalist, allowed Rorty to take command of the battery. See also: Personal Military Records of James M. Rorty, Albert Sheldon, and Henry Rosegrant (Washington, D.C., NNRG-NA).

³Colonel McGilvery simply reported that the

unidentified volunteer battery had disappeared.

⁴Probably the 2nd Maine Battery then in position east of and above both Zeigler's Grove and Taneytown Road. Gate's two regiments belonging to Biddle advanced north of the 13th Vermont and were not part of the line engaged between the Hummelbaugh and Trostle farm lanes. Thus, they should not be considered part of the Plum Run Line.

⁵*OR*, 351. Munson's five companies would in time become the right wing of the regiment while those with Randall would be the left wing.

⁶*Ibid.*

⁷*Ibid.*

⁸*Ibid.* After leaving Randall, Doubleday found Stannard east of the road at his headquarters. Ordering the 14th and 16th Vermont to their feet, he led them out of the Guinn swale onto the Taneytown Road. As they passed Meade's headquarters General Meade joined them.

⁹*Ibid.*

¹⁰Hancock to Bachelder. Letter from Governors Island , New York. November 7, 1885. *BP*, 2:1134.

¹¹*OR*, 352.

¹²*OR,* 543. Colonel Gates's 80th New York advanced to the right of the 13th Vermont, away from Plum Run, and should not be included as one of the regiments that fought along its length. Also following, the 16th and 14th Vermont Volunteers advanced as had Gates, north of the 13th.

¹³*Ibid.*

¹⁴*OR*, 501. Weir's three guns were returned to the ridge

by Col. Calvin Craig, 105th Pennsylvania. First Brigade, First Division, Third Corps, using men from his and Brewster's commands.

[15]*OR,* Pt. 2, 629.

[16]*Ibid.* Moffett. Colonel Randall mistakenly claimed this limbered piece as a Confederate prize.

[17]*Ibid.*

[18]*OR*, 352. There were no Confederate field pieces, limbers, and or caissons reported missing that day.

[19]*Ibid.*

Chapter 19

[1] Sunset was 7:32 P.M.

[2] Moonrise was 8:38 P.M. The moon was 99% full.

[3] July 4th, 1863: Return of Casualties in the Union forces, commanded by Maj. Gen. George G. Meade, U.S. Army at the Battle of Gettysburg, Pa., July First-3, 1863. (Washington D.C. NNRG-NA.) see also *OR*, 174. Personal Military Records of James Miles. (Washington DC. NNRG-NA) hereafter cited as *OR Pt. I*. Returns.

[4] *OR*, 345 and 348. Both regiments were probably involved with Livington's guns in one way or another.

[5] *Ibid.*, 559 Brewster incorrectly suggested his line was relieved by a brigade from the Second Corps when in fact he was probably referring to the 19th Maine and or 13th Vermont, or possibly Dana's three regiments.

6 *Ibid.*

7 The sun rose at 4:36 a.m.

8 Adolpho F. de la Cabada [Cavada] Diary, 1861-1863 Entry dated July 2-3, 1863, Historical Society of Pennsylvania, Philadelphia, Pa.

9 Busey, *Those Honored Dead*, 140-145.

10*Ibid.* See also *OR Vol. I Pt. I,* Returns, 189-192

11 Charles Carpenter letter home, dated July 3, 1863, as noted in Holcomb, *First Minnesota*, 347.

12 Lymen Pierce, *The First Minnesota at Gettysburg* (Mankato, Minnesota: Mankato State College, 1959), 23-25.

13 *Ibid.* Marvin was assisted to an aide station in rear of Thomas by another wounded soldier from the 1st Minnesota

14 Patrick Taylor diary entry-July Second, as noted in Holcomb, *First Minnesota*, 346. See also Gregory A. Coco, *A Vast Sea of Misery: A History Guide to the Union and Confederate Field Hospitals at Gettysburg. July First-November 20, 1863* (Gettysburg, Pa.: Thomas Publications. 1988), 75 (hereafter cited as *Vast Sea of Misery*). Pvt. Isaac Taylor's corpse was identified on July Third.

15 Charles Carpenter letter home, dated July Third, 1863, as noted in Holcomb, *First Minnesota*, 34 See also: Coco, *Vast Sea of Misery*, 75

16 Smith, *History of the 19th Maine*, 72-73. .

17 *Ibid.*

18 *Ibid.*

19 *Ibid.*

Chapter 20

[1] Dana assumed command after Stone was wounded.

[2] Watson's artillerists were all Regulars, as opposed to Volunteers, hence regular guns.

[3] *OR*, 429. Placing a second tin of canister in the tube [Double Canister] would physically double the number of canister rounds fired, thus increasing the total amount of ordnance claimed on the returns.

[4] *Ibid.*, 372

[5] Seven Federal batteries, or portions thereof, were overrun July Second with the loss of 22 field pieces. All but three would be recaptured.

[6] Hunt to Ransom, September 1880, Hunt Papers.

Epilogue

[1] Meinhard, *GBM*, 81. The exact number of men in the July Second charge is questionable. Company C, numbering 32, and Company L (2nd Minnesota Sharpshooters), numbering 56, had been detached as skirmishers West of the Copse of Trees. In a letter to Colonel Bachelder, dated June 9, 1866, Colvill estimates the number at 262. Total number effective was 330. The numbers are too close to assume Colvill wrong. See Busey & Martin, *Regimental Strengths and Losses*, 39. June 30 muster is 399 with effective at Gettysburg numbering 330.

[2] *Ibid.*

[3] Coddington, *The Gettysburg Campaign*, 422–424. Col. George L Willard's Third Brigade belonged to Brig. Gen. Alexander Hays's Third Division, Second Corps.

[4] Holcombe, *1st Minnesota*, 343–344.

[5] Eric Campbell, "'Remember Harpers Ferry': The Degradation, Humiliation, And Redemption of Col. George L. Willard's Brigade," *GBM* 7 (1992), 51 and 54–58, which provides a superb, detailed overview of the Harpers Ferry ordeal and the rebuilding of the regiments in Willard's Brigade.

[6] Coddington, *The Gettysburg Campaign,* 423.

[7] Richardson to Bachelder, *BP,* 1:338-339.

Appendix

[1] Shultz & Rollins, "Measuring Pickett's Charge," *GBM, Issue Number 17,* July, 1997 p. 115. The elongated ridge paralleling the Emmitsburg Road, referred to as the Emmitsburg Road Rise, is 580 feet above sea level, roughly 20 feet higher than both Cemetery and Seminary Ridge, and 30 feet higher than Plum Run.

[2] *Ibid.*

[3] United States Geological Survey Topographical Satellite Image, Gettysburg: Map 39077–G2–TF. The spring feeding Plum Run is much like that of Spangler's Spring located near Culp's Hill, the difference being the quality and quantity of water. See also History and Records of Camp Cole,

United States Adjutant Generals Office, National Archives, Washington, D.C.

⁴*Ibid.* The small fist shaped knoll is a low extension of Cemetery Ridge jutting west above Plum Run. It's northern base is about 40 yards south of the present day left flank marker of the 1st Minnesota located in Plum Run Ravine.

⁵*Ibid.*

Bibliography

Primary Sources:

Newspapers & Magazines:

Boston Sunday Herald
Confederate Veteran. 40 vols. Nashville, Tenn., 1893-1932
Kennebec Journal
Gettysburg Compiler
Gettysburg Star & Sentinel
Historical Magazine, Series Two
National Tribune
New York Herald
New York Times
Minneapolis Journal
Philadelphia Inquirer
Philadelphia Weekly Times
Portland Advertiser
The Times (London)
Winona Post

Manuscript Materials:
Special Collections:

Duke University. W. R. Perkins Library, Special Collections and Manuscript Department, Durham, N.C:

James Longstreet Papers

Georgia Historical Society, Savannah, Ga.:

William P. Pigman Papers

Gettysburg National Military Park. Gettysburg, Pa.:

Benjamin W. Thompson Notes

Charles A. Richardson Papers

Hugo Hilderbrandt Papers

United States Battlefield Commission, "A Record of the Position of Troops at Gettysburg."

Uriel C. Bells Papers

Gulian V. Weir Letters

Manuscripts Division, Library of Congress, Washington, D.C.:

Cadmus R. Wilcox Papers

Henry J. Hunt Papers

Revere Family Papers

Mississippi State Department of Archives and History. Jackson, Miss.:

Ethelbert Barksdale Papers, "Barksdale's Mississippi Brigade at Gettysburg"

New Hampshire Historical Society, Concord, N.H.:

John B. Bachelder Papers

The Historical Society of Pennsylvania. Philadelphia, Pa.:

Adolpho F. de la Cabada (Cavada) Diary, 1861-63.

Andrew A. Humphreys Papers

John Gibbon Papers

National Archives and Records Administration, Washington, D.C.:

Record Group 92, records of the Office of the

Confederacy

Record Group 94, records of the Office of the Adjutant General

Record Group 153, records of the Office of the Judge Advocate General

The Southern Historical Society Papers, Richmond, Va.:

David Lang Letter to Edward Perry, July 19, 1863.

The Huntington Library, Rare Books & Manuscripts Division. San Marino, Cal.:

John P. Nicholson Collection

The Ontario County, New York Historical Society, Canandaigua, N.Y.:

Charles Richardson Letters

The New York Historical Society, New York, N.Y.:

Abner Doubleday Papers

Special Collection, Orlando Public Library, Orlando, Fla.:

David Lang Letters

Special Collections & Manuscript Department, United States Army Military History Institute, Carlisle, Pa.:

Robert L. Brake Collection

A. A. Humphreys Papers

Regimental Vertical Files

Library and Special Collections Department, The United States Military Academy at West Point, West Point, N.Y.:

Weir Family Papers

Evan Thomas Papers

Published Primary Sources:

Adams. John R. *Reminiscences of the Nineteenth Massachusetts Regiment*. Boston: Wright & Potter Printing Company, 1899.

Adams, Silas. "The Nineteenth Maine at Gettysburg." Military Order of the United States, Maine Commandery, *War Papers 4*, 1915: 249-263.

Babcock, Nathan. "The 114th Regiment, Pennsylvania Volunteers." *Philadelphia Weekly Times*, April 24, 1886.

Bandy, Kenneth, & Florence Freeland, comp. *The Gettysburg Papers*. Two vols. Dayton: Morningside Publishing House Inc., 1978.

Bartlett, A. W. *The History of the Twelfth New Hampshire Volunteers In The War Of The Rebellion*. Concord, N. H.: Ira C. Evans, Printer, 1886.

Bigelow, John, Jr., *The Peach Orchard, Gettysburg, July 2, 1863*. Minneapolis: Kimball-Storer, 1910.

Chamberlin, Thomas, ed. *History of the One Hundred and Fiftieth Regiment Pennsylvania Volunteers*. Philadelphia: J. B. Lippincott Company, 1895.

Clark, George. "Wilcox's Alabama Brigade at Gettysburg." *Confederate Veteran* 17 (1909): 229-230.

Cleaves, Freeman. *Meade of Gettysburg*. Norman, Ok.: University of Oklahoma Press, 1960.

Dana, Charles A. *Recollections of the Civil War*. New York: Appelton & Company, 1902.

Fleming, George T., ed. "Alexander Hays at the Battle of Gettysburg," *The Life and Letters of Alexander Hays.* Pittsburgh, Pa.: Compiled by Gilbert Hays, 1913.

Fortin, Maurice S. ed. "Colonel Hilary A. Herbert's 'History of the 8th Alabama Volunteer Regiment, C. S. A.'" *Alabama Historical Quarterly* 39 (1977): 5-321.

Groene, Bertram. ed., "Civil War Letters of Colonel David Lang." *Florida Historical Quarterly* 54 (1976): 340-348.

Hale, Charles A. "Gettysburg: The Work Being Done By The Battlefield Memorial Association." *National Tribune,* September 11, 1884.

Hancock, Almira Russell. *Reminiscences of Winfield Scott Hancock.* New York: Charles L. Webster and Company, 1887.

Hanifen, Michael. ed., *History of Battery B, First New Jersey Artillery.* Ottawa, Ill.: Republican Times Printing Company, 1905.

Herbert, Hilary A. "Colonel Hilary A. Herbert's History of the Eighth Alabama Volunteer Regiment, C.S.A." *Alabama Historical Quarterly* 39 (1977): 115- 200.

Holcombe. Return I. *History of the First Regiment, Minnesota Volunteers.* Stillwater, Minn.: Easton and Masterman, 1916.

Hunt, Henry J. "The Second Day at Gettysburg." Included in Robert O. Johnson and C. C. Buel, eds. *Battles and Leaders of the Civil War.* 4 vols. (New York: Century Publishing Company, 1884-1888): 3: 278-296.

Ladd, David L. and Audrey J., eds. *The Bachelder Papers: Gettysburg in Their Own Words*. 3 vols. Dayton: Morningside House, Inc. 1995.

Lang, David. "Letter to General Edward Perry, July, 19, 1863: Gettysburg, The Courageous Part Taken in the Desperate Conflict., 2-3 July, 1863., by the Florida Brigade." *Southern Historical Society Papers* 27 (1889): 79-88.

Lochren, William. "The First Minnesota at Gettysburg." In *Military Order of the Loyal Legion of the United States, Minnesota Commandery, Glimpses of the Nation's Struggle, Series Three* (1890): 42-56.

Love, William. "Mississippi at Gettysburg." *Mississippi Historical Society Papers*, Series Nine. (1906): 25-51.

McNeily, J.S. "Barksdale's Brigade at Gettysburg: Most Magnificent Charge of the War" Mississippi Historical Society Papers, Series Nineteen, 1914.

Maine at Gettysburg Commission. *Maine at Gettysburg: Report of the Maine Commissioners*. Portland, Me.: Lakeside Press, 1898.

Meade, George Jr. *With Meade at Gettysburg*. Philadelphia, Pa.: Winston Company, Inc., 1930.

New York Monuments Commission for the Battlefields of Gettysburg and Chattanooga. *Final Report on the Battlefield of Gettysburg* (New York at Gettysburg Three Volumes). Albany: Lyon Company Printers, 1900.
42nd Regiment. New York: Tammany Printers, 1892.
111th Regiment. Canandaigua, N. Y.: Times Book & Printing House, 1886.

126th Regiment. Canandaigua: Times Book & Printing House, 1888.

Pennsylvania at Gettysburg: Ceremonies at the Dedication of the Monuments Erected by the Commonwealth of Pennsylvania to Maj. Gen. George Gordon Meade, Maj. Gen. Winfield Scott Hancock, Maj. Gen. John Fulton Reynolds, and to Mark the Positions of the Pennsylvania Commands Engaged in the Battle. Harrisburg: William S. Ray, State Printer, 1939.

Purcell, Hugh D. "The Nineteenth Massachusetts at Gettysburg." *Essex Institute Historical Collection.* 1963.

Rhodes, John H. *The History of Battery B, First Regiment Rhode Island Light Artillery.* Providence: Snow and Farnham Printers, 1914.

Scott, George H. "Vermont at Gettysburg." Included in James McLean, Jr. and Judy W. McLean, eds. *Gettysburg Sources, Volume I.* Baltimore: Butternut and Blue, 1986: 72-73.

Seventy-Fifth Anniversary of the Battle of Gettysburg. Report of the Pennsylvania Commission. Gettysburg Times and News Publishing Company, 1939.

Simons, Ezra D. *A Regimental History: The One Hundred and Twenty-fifth New York State Volunteers.* New York: Judson Printing Company, 1888.

Smith, John D. *The History of the Nineteenth Regiment of Maine Volunteers Infantry, 1862-1865.* Minneapolis, Minn.: Great Western Printing Company, 1909.

Tremain, Henry E. *Two Days of War. A Gettysburg Narrative*

and Other Experiences. New York: Silver's and Bowers Booksellers, 1905.

United States Congress. *Report of the Joint Committee on the Conduct of the War at the Second Session, Thirty-Eighth Congress, Army of the Potomac.* Washington D.C.: United States Government Printing Office, 1865.

United States War Department. *The War of the Rebellion: A Compilation of the Official records of the Union and Confederate Armies.* 128 vols. in 3 series. Washington, D.C.: United States Government Printing Office, 1880-1901.

Waitt, Ernest L. *History of the Nineteenth Regiment, Massachusetts Volunteer Infantry.* Salem, Mass.: 1906.

Walker. Francis A. *History of the Second Army Corps.* New York, N.Y. Charles Scribner's Sons, 1886.

Ward. Joseph R. C. History of the *One-Hundred and Sixth Regiment, Pennsylvania Volunteers.* Philadelphia: Grant, Faires & Rogers, 1883.

Weygant, Charles H. *History of the One Hundred and twenty-fourth Regiment, New York State Volunteers.* Newburg, N.Y.: Journal Printing House, 1977.

Wilcox, Cadmus M. "General C. M. Wilcox on the Battle of Gettysburg." *Southern Historical Society Papers* 6(1878): 97-124.

Secondary Sources:

Burns, James A. "The 12th New Hampshire Regiment At Gettysburg and Beyond." *Gettysburg Magazine* 20 (June, 1999): 116-118 (hereafter cited as GBM).

Busey, John W., and David Martin. *Regimental Strengths and Losses at Gettysburg.* Baltimore: Gateway Press,1982.

Campbell, Eric. "Caldwell Clears The Wheatfield." GBM 3 (July 1990): 27-33.

------------------. "Remember Harpers Ferry: The Degradation, Humiliation, and Redemption of Col. George L. Willard's Brigade." GBM 7 (July 1992): 51-75.

Coddington, Edwin B. *The Gettysburg Campaign: A Study in Command.* New York: Charles Scribner's Sons, 1968.

Dickenson, Christopher C. "Col. Francis Voltaire Randall And The 13th Vermont Infantry." GBM 17 (July 1998): 83-102.

Downs, David B. 'His Left Was Worth a Glance: Meade and the Union Left on July 2, 1863." GBM 7 (July 1992): 34-39.

Elmore, Thomas L. "The Florida Brigade At Gettysburg." GBM 15 (January, 1997): 45-53.

Gottfried, Bradley M. "Wright's Charge On July 2, 1863: Piercing The Union Line Or Inflated Glory" GBM 17 (January 1998): 70-81.

Hadden , Lee. "The Granite Glory: The 19th Maine At

Gettysburg." GBM 13 (July 1995): 50-52.

Heiser, John. "Action On The Emmitsburg Road." GBM 1 (July 1989): 79-85

Hess, Earl J. *The Union Soldier in Battle: Enduring the Ordeal of Combat.* Lawrence, Kan.: University of Kansas Press, 1997.

Imholt, John Q. *The First Volunteers: History of the First Minnesota Volunteer Regiment.* Minneapolis: Ross and Haines, 1963.

Lochren, William. "Narrative of the First Minnesota." *Minnesota in the Civil and Indian Wars, 1861-1865.* (1891): 2:33-35.

Meinhard, Robert W. "The First Minnesota At Gettysburg." GBM 5 (July 1991): 79-88.

Pfanz, Harry W. "From Bloody Battlefield to Historic Shrine." *Civil War Times* 2 (July 1963): 39-41.

-------------------. *Gettysburg: The Second Day.* Chapel Hill: University of North Carolina Press, 1987.

Rauss, Edmund Jr. *A Generation on the March: The Union Army at Gettysburg.* Lynchburg, Va.: H. E. Howard, Inc., 1987.

Reese, Timothy J. *Sykes' Regular Infantry Division, 1861-1864: A History of Regular United States Infantry Operations in the Civil War's Eastern Theater.* Jefferson, N. C.: McFarland Co., 1990.

Rollins, Richard, David Shultz. "Measuring Pickett's Charge." GBM 17 (January, 1998): 108-117.

Shultz, David L. "Gulian V. Weir's 5th U.S. Artillery, Battery C."

GBM 18 (July 1998): 82-88.

Tucker, Glen. *Hancock the Superb.* Indianapolis: Bobbs-Merrill Company, 1960.

Woods, James A. "Defending Watson's Battery" GBM 9 (January, 1994): 41-47.

----------------------. "Humphreys' Division's Flank March to Little Round Top." GBM 6 (January 1992): 59-61

Winschel, Terrence L. "Their Supreme Moment: Barksdale's Brigade At Gettysburg." GBM 1 (July 1989): 70-77.

Williamson, Edward. "Francis P. Fleming in the War for Southern Independence, Letters from the Front." *Florida Historical Quarterly* 28 (October, 1949): 145-147.

Index

Adams, Lt. Col. John, 106

Adams, Sgt. Silas, 29, 62, 65, 142

Alabama Military Units; *8th Infantry,* 90, 92-93, 95-99, 102-103, 107-108, (tour) 203, 225, 229-230; *9th Infantry,* 66, 72, 80, 86, 93, 95, 98, 108-109, 112; *10th Infantry,* 87-90, 95, 100-103, 107-108, (tour) 204, 226; *11th Infantry,* 87-93, 95-96, 98-99, 102-103, 107-108, (tour) 226, 229; *14th Infantry,* 66, 80, 86, 90, 93, 98, 108-109

Alexander, Col. E. Porter, 76, 117

Angle, the, (tour) 233

Arnold, Capt. William A. (1st Rhode Island Light Artillery, Battery A, 13, 26-27; *Arnold's Battery,* 13-16, 19, 25, 36, 46, (tour) 196-197

Baldwin, Col. Clark, 50

Baldwin, Lt. Homer, 82-83, 85

Baltimore Pike, 8-10, 36, 93, 244n, (tour) 177, 215

Baltimore, Maryland, 5, 9

Barksdale, Gen. William, 55, 103, 154, (tour) 236-237, 240, *photo,* 73; *Barksdale's Brigade;* 55, 72, 78, 87, 90, 94, 103-104, 116-118, 147, 153-156, 159, 169, 256n, 261n, (tour) 199, 202-205, 208, 210, 214-215, 235-240

Barnes's (Gen. James) Division, 45

Humphreys, Col. Benjamin G., 104-105, 117, 146-147, 153

Hunt, Gen. Henry J., 12, 38-39, 42, 44, 47, 51, 84, 151, 243n, 244n, 254n, 264n

Indiana Military Units; *14th Infantry,* 6, *15th Infantry,* 242n

Irish Brigade, 47, 116, 121, (tour) 212

Irish, Capt. Nathaniel, 84

Irvin, Capt. John, 133

Jackson, Gen. Thomas J., 16

James, Lt. Robert, 63-65, 71, 83-85, 119, 146, 148-149, (tour) 214, 224

Jones, Capt. George W., 133

Jones, Pvt. Israel D., 28

Kelly, Col. Patrick, 252n

Kemper's (Gen. James) Brigade, (tour) 225, 234

Kershaw's (Gen. Joseph) Brigade, (tour) 236-239

Ketchum, Col. John H., 118

Klingle farm and house, 36, 59, 66, 87, 101, 114, 130, 149, 155, 168, 170, 250n, (tour) 198, 200, 204, 202, 206-207, 220, 224-225, 235-236, 240

Lakeman, Col. Moses, 255n

Peach Orchard, the Sherfy, xii, 15-16, 30, 37, 45, 49, 53, 55,
        76, 100-101, 115, 117, 151, 154, 250n, (tour) 209, 213,
        237-240, *photo,* 196
Peeples, Lt. Samuel, 104, 152
Pennsylvania Military Units; *1st Artillery, Battery C
        (Thompson),* 145, 147; *16th Cavalry,* (tour) 176; *26th
        Infantry,* 88, 145, (tour) 206; *69th Infantry,* (tour)
        239; *71st Infantry,* 27, 30-31, 46, 56; *72nd Infantry,*
        27, 31, 46, 56; *105th Infantry,* 145, 265n; *106th Infan-
        try,* 29, (tour) 196; *143rd Infantry,* 120, 133, 144, 160;
        149th Infantry, 120, 133-134, 144, 160; *150th Infan-
        try,* 120, 133, 144, 160; *151st Infantry,* 120; *Artillery,
        Independent, Battery C & F,* (tour) 222
Periam, Capt. Joseph, 106
Phillips, Capt. Charles A. (5th Massachusetts Artillery), 145,
        (tour) 213; *Phillips's Battery,* 116, 118, 147, 262n
Pickett's Charge, 1, 148
Pleasonton Avenue, (tour) 179, 183, 184-187, 190, 195, 207,
        222-223
Plum Run, 11, 36-37, 39-41, 44, 49, 55, 59-66, 70, 72-73,
        75-76, 78-79, 86-89, 95-102, 104, 106-110, 112, 114,
        116-119, 126, 130-131, 134-136, 138-139, 141, 144-145,
        147, 149-150, 153-154, 157, 160, 167-171, 265n, 269n,
        270n, (tour) 174, 191-193, 198, 202-203, 205-209, 213-
        217, 220-230, 236, 238, 240, *photo,* 194, 229
Porter, Pvt. John, 82

Randall, Col. Francis V., 122-130, 132, 265n-266n, (tour) 193

Ransom, Capt. Dunbar R., 4-9, 12, 49-50, 98, 143, 243n, 245n-246n, 253n, 256n, (tour) 180, 186-189, 206, 234

Rhode Island Military Units; *1st Light Artillery, Battery A (Arnold),* 13-14, 19; *1st Light Artillery, Battery B (Brown),* 21, 25-26, 46, 258n; *1st Light Artillery, Battery E* (Bucklyn), 253n

Richardson, Capt. Charles, 248n-249n

Riddle, Pvt. James, 81

Roemer, Lt. Jacob, 83

Rogers farm, 40, (tour) 226, 234

Rorty, Capt. James M. (1st New York, Battery B), 120-122, 145, 253n, 264n

Rose house and woods, 47, 53, (tour) 239

Rosegrant, Pvt. Henry, 121

Ross, Maj. (-), 128

Ruger's (Gen. Thomas H.) Brigade, 119

Schriber, Michael (farm), 7, (tour) 186

Seeley, Capt. Aaron P. (4th U. S. Artillery, Battery K), 63-64, 80, 87, 89, 146, 248n, (tour) 200, 202, 204, 234, 240; *Seeley's Battery,* 63, 87, 100, 119, 146, 148, 261n-262n, (tour) 200, 202, 204, 215, 235

Seminary Ridge, 13, 24-25, 40, 53, 155, 269n, (tour) 188, 233

Semmes's (Gen. Paul) Brigade, (tour) 236-237

Sharrow, Pvt. Peter, 82

Sheldon, Lt. Albert (1st New York Artillery, Battery B), 33-